The Digital Divide

The Digital Divide

JAN VAN DIJK

polity

First published in 2020 by Polity Press

Polity Press
65 Bridge Street
Cambridge CB2 1UR, UK

Polity Press
101 Station Landing
Suite 300
Medford, MA 02155, USA

ISBN-13: 978-1-5095-3444-9
ISBN-13: 978-1-5095-3445-6 (pb)

A catalogue record for this book is available from the British Library.

Library of Congress Cataloging-in-Publication Data

Names: Dijk, Jan van, 1952- author.
Title: The digital divide / Jan van Dijk.
Description: Cambridge, UK ; Medford, MA : Polity, 2019. | Includes
    bibliographical references and index. | Summary: "Contrary to optimistic
    visions of a free internet for all, the problem of the 'digital divide'
    has persisted for close to twenty-five years. Jan van Dijk considers the
    state of digital inequality and what we can do to tackle it"-- Provided
    by publisher.
Identifiers: LCCN 2019023991 (print) | LCCN 2019023992 (ebook) | ISBN
    9781509534449 (hardback) | ISBN 9781509534456 (paperback) | ISBN
    9781509534463 (epub)
Subjects: LCSH: Digital divide. | Computer literacy. | Internet literacy. |
    Equality.
Classification: LCC HM851 .D56 2019 (print) | LCC HM851 (ebook) | DDC
    303.48/33--dc23
LC record available at https://lccn.loc.gov/2019023991
LC ebook record available at https://lccn.loc.gov/2019023992

Typeset in 11 on 13pt Adobe Garamond Pro by
Servis Filmsetting Ltd, Stockport, Cheshire
Printed and bound in Great Britain by CPI Group (UK) Ltd, Croydon

For further information on Polity, visit our website:
politybooks.com

Contents

Acknowledgements

This book is a result of twenty-five years of research on the digital divide by me and others. Fifteen years ago I summarized my first thoughts about this topic in *The Deepening Divide: Inequality in the Information Society* (2005). At first sight this book looks similar. In fact, it is quite different, because here the assumptions of the former volume are tested in a large number of surveys, experiments and analyses of official statistics. The resources and appropriation theory I sketched previously has matured and is elaborated here. This book covers not only the so-called first-level digital divide research of that time (concerning physical access) but also the second level (digital skills and usage) and the third level (the outcomes of using or not using digital media). However, the inconvenient message is new: that digital inequality reinforces existing social inequality.

The framework of *The Digital Divide* is broad enough to summarize not only my own work and that of my staff since 2005 but also that of others. This is the first textbook on the digital divide aimed at those in higher education, especially in the social sciences and media courses covering the social aspects of digital media, and the numerous figures, tables and lists render the results accessible to all.

I am very grateful to those who have read earlier drafts and made useful comments, in particular Professor Alexander van Deursen, with whom I have collaborated on several articles and a book on digital skills. I am also indebted to the reviewers at Polity Press for their suggestions.

Finally, I want to thank my wife Ineke for her patience, support and love while her now officially retired husband 'is working harder than ever before'.

1   What is the Digital Divide?

Introduction: the concept of the digital divide

In the year 2020 both the concept of and the research into the digital divide will be twenty-five years old. In 1995 the term 'digital divide' was first used in a number of newspapers in the United States. It was backed by data in the report *Falling through the Net*, published by the National Telecommunications and Information Administration, which talked about 'haves and have nots' (NTIA 1995). Soon the concept spread to Europe and the rest of the world, and by the millennium both the idea and the problematic of the digital divide were firmly established on the societal and scholarly agenda.

But what does the concept actually mean? It has produced so many definitions, controversies and misunderstandings that several people were in favour of discarding it after a few years (Compaine 2001; Gunkel 2003). The most common definition runs as follows: *a division between people who have access and use of digital media and those who do not.* The term '*access*' was emphasized in the first years of discourse, though later the word '*use*' was highlighted.

A common synonym for digital media is the general term 'information and communication technology'. Access can refer to its devices, connections or applications. The first device to be accessed was a stand-alone computer or a PC, to be followed by a series of digital media, both mobile (mobile phones, laptops, tablets and smartphones) and digitized analogue media (television, radio, cameras and game devices). Connections mentioned were the Internet, mobile telephony and digital broadcasting, with either narrow- or broadcasting capacities. Finally, the applications of most interest were e-mail, search engines, e-commerce, e-banking and social-networking sites.

Before the concept of the digital divide, other terms were used, mostly related to the concepts of the information society and (in)equality: information inequality (Schiller 1981, 1996), knowledge gap (Tichenor et al. 1970) and participation in the information society (Lyon 1988). Access and use became linked to digital skills or literacy, motivation ('want-nots') and such outcomes as a democratic divide and an economic opportunity divide (Mossberger et al. 2003).

Table 1.1. Definitions of the digital divide

Type	Definition
General	A division between people who have access to and use of digital media and those who do not
Specific	• WHO (individuals vs. organizations/communities vs. societies/ countries/regions), • with WHICH characteristics (*individuals*: income, education, age, gender; *organizations*: public or private ownership, size, sector; *countries*: developed or developing, urban or rural) connects • HOW (access, skills, usage) • to WHAT type of technology (computer, Internet, phone, digital TV)? (Hilbert 2011a)
Process	Divisions in the access to and use of four phases in the adoption of digital media: motivation, physical access, digital skills and usage

In this book I will offer my own framework of four phases of access and use of digital media in order to understand better the concept of the digital divide: motivation, physical access, skills and usage. A descriptive framework is offered by Hilbert (2011a: 19), who defines the digital divide by answering four specific questions (see table 1.1).

We will see that the focus of digital divide research is, first, on individuals and, second, on divisions between countries or within countries (urban and rural). There has also been attention paid to the individual demographics and characteristics of countries (rich and poor or developed or developing). The short history of the discourse below shows that the emphasis on 'how' runs from access to skills and usage. Finally, the technology in question has moved from PCs and dial-up or narrowcast Internet to hand-held computers, mobile devices and broadband Internet.

The dangers of a metaphor

The term 'digital divide' is a metaphor. A metaphor is a vivid figure of speech applying a word or phrase to something to which it is not literally applicable. In English, a *divide* is both a point or a line of division – a specific term indicating a geographical dividing line, such as a watershed. In other languages, *digital divide* is also defined in metaphorical terms, such as an opening (*brecha* in Spanish), a gorge (*Kluft* in German) or a fracture (*fracture numérique* in French). Thus the digital divide also indicates a social split between people in a divided society. Here the distinction *inclusion in or exclusion from society* is relevant.

The metaphor has also caused a number of misconceptions. The first misunderstanding is that the digital divide is a simple division between two clearly separated social categories. However, because in contemporary societies we exhibit an increasingly multifaceted social, economic and cultural variation, it is more helpful to see it as a range of positions extending across whole populations – from people having no access and use at all to those with full access and using several applications every day. If any delineation is required, a tripartite society might be a better definition than a two-tiered one. At one extreme we perceive an information elite and at the other the digitally illiterate or the fully excluded. In between are the majority of the population, having access in one way or another and using digital technology to a certain extent (see van Dijk [1999] 2012, 2000).

The second misconception is that this gap cannot be closed and that it will lead to structural or persisting inequality. It has been shown that this is not the case in terms of physical access to digital technology – a bridge that has been crossed in the developed countries. Bridging different skills and usage opportunities might be more difficult. However, in this book I will show that these differences can also be mitigated by sensible policies of governments, businesses, educational institutions, and consumers or citizens.

A third misconception is the assumption that the digital divide is about absolute inequality, as it is often framed in the concepts 'inclusion' in and 'exclusion' from society. In fact, all types of access to digital technology discussed in this book are relative distinctions. As different people have different degrees of motivation, physical access, skills and usage opportunities leading to different outcomes, as well as different levels of support, a relational and network view of inequality will be discussed.

A fourth danger of the metaphor is that it suggests a single digital divide. In fact the actual state of digital inequality is much more complex (van Dijk and Hacker 2003) and is linked to existing social, economic and cultural divisions in society.

Finally, the term 'digital' suggests that the digital divide is a technical issue when, in fact, it is more of a social problem. Technical properties of digital media are important for access and use – they can be complicated or relatively simple – but the causes and effects of (in)equality are social. The digital divide is not brought to an end when everybody owns and commands the technology concerned. In this book I argue that the digital divide is here to stay even when all such problems are overcome.

Is the digital divide special?

Some people question whether the phenomenon of the digital divide is new or special. Society has seen the introduction of many problematical technologies. How is the introduction of digital media different from that of compulsory reading and writing in the nineteenth and twentieth centuries, for example? This question can be answered from several perspectives. We might look to the *innovation*, the acceptance and the development of new technology by individuals and societies. The phenomenon can also be framed in terms of *(in)equality*, when some people have more opportunities to adopt and use new technology than others. A third perspective is the effect of the introduction of this technology for people and society in terms of *participation* (see table 1.2): in which respects are people more or less included in or excluded from society?

In terms of innovation, acceptance and development, information and communication technology created after the Second World War was introduced relatively speedily, in about a generation. It was even called a 'digital revolution'. The majority of the population took to particular media and applications pretty quickly, first of all in the developed countries. The World Wide Web, created in 1993, was already in use in the vast majority of these countries after fifteen years. The uptake of social media, starting in 2004, showed the fastest adoption rate of any mass medium in history. About 2 billion people in the world became Facebook users in only ten to twelve years. The 'digital revolution' happened so fast that it is not surprising that large numbers of people, especially in the developing countries, lagged behind and so led to a digital divide.

The digital divide is framed primarily in terms of (in)equality. The question is whether it is special in this respect in comparison with former technologies or media. This depends on the aspect of (in)equality we are considering: as Amartya Sen asked, 'Equality of *what?*' (Sen 1992: ix). Is

Table 1.2. Perspectives on the digital divide

Perspective	Description
Innovation	Adoption or not of information and communication technology for progress or development
(In)equality	More or fewer opportunities to adopt and use information and communication technology
Participation in society	Inclusion in or exclusion from society by adopting and using information and communication technology

it (in)equality of opportunities, life chances, freedoms, capital, resources, positions, capabilities, skills? Unfortunately, the answer is not made clear in most books and articles about the digital divide. In this book I will refer to all of these aspects or expressions of (in)equality. A special characteristic of the digital divide in terms of (in)equality is that, more than was the case with former technologies, it touches every imaginable part of society. The main reason is that digital media are used in all types of activities in daily life, while for example reading books or newspapers and watching television are only mental activities (see chapter 6).

One of the main aspects of the digital divide is inequality of capabilities or skills. This is often linked to the concept of 'literacy'. We often read about a comparison between digital and traditional literacy. Is digital literacy different from the traditional literacy of reading and writing? There are many similarities between the two, but there also are differences in skills required (van Dijk and van Deursen 2014; van Deursen and van Dijk 2016). On the one hand, digital media simplify the finding of information – for example, using a search engine would seem to be easier than consulting a library catalogue or index cards. On the other hand, digital media are also more complicated: they require new and special skills in the use of search engines.

The third perspective of the digital divide is in terms of participation – whether individuals are included in or excluded from society in such domains as work, education, the market, community, citizenship, politics and culture. Is the access to and use of digital media more important for participation in these domains than the access to and use of print media, television, radio and the telephone? My answer in this book is that they are even more important. ICTs are general-purpose technologies. While older technologies are important for knowledge, entertainment or communication, digital media are used for every act, purpose or need in society. Increasingly, access to and use of digital media is needed to participate as a worker, entrepreneur, student, consumer or citizen, or in any other role in contemporary society. In this respect the digital divide is special too.

Is the digital divide a problem for society?

Nevertheless, it has to be demonstrated that people can no longer play any other role in contemporary society without using digital technology. In many ways, printed media, television, radio and the telephone are still working in apparently satisfactory ways. However, in this book we will see that, increasingly, access to and use of digital media is needed at least to enjoy all benefits in society. In most developed countries governments

Table 1.3. Perspectives of the digital divide as a problem

Perspective	Problem
Innovation and economic growth	Lack of innovation, development and economic growth of a country
Inequality and exclusion	Economic, social and cultural inequality and exclusion of people from society
Security	People without access are a security risk for society because they cannot be kept under surveillance by governments and by businesses.

expect that citizens have an e-mail address and access to the Internet. More and more jobs require digital skills at a particular level. You cannot take advantage of education without being able to use a computer and the Internet. Without using social-networking sites people may lose friends or contacts and miss invitations for parties and the like. A lack of fast digital connections may lead to people finding that concerts and festivals are sold out. So the digital divide is increasingly a problem for society. Here again the perspective is threefold (see table 1.3).

International institutions such as the UN, the International Tele-communication Union (ITU), the OECD and the World Bank frame the digital divide primarily as a socio-economic indicator for growth and development. Their reports reveal strong correlations between the number of Internet connections and ICT use in a country and its rate of development, innovation and economic growth (see a summary in the report of the World Bank (2016), with its telling title *Digital Dividends*). From this perspective, governments and international economic bodies and technical institutions (such as the ITU) see the digital divide primarily as a matter of economic policy and international competition. In developed countries, the digital divide limits the innovative capacity of an economy because a proportion of the population cannot keep up. In developing countries, it impedes economic growth and the capacity to keep pace with the developed countries.

The second perspective, which prevails in social and media or communication science, is a social one: (in)equality and inclusion in or exclusion from society. Here the main question is whether the digital divide is a byproduct of old inequalities or whether it is a new inequality. This is also one of the most important questions I ask in this book. Does the digital divide intensify existing inequalities or does it cause new ones? It is often claimed that inequality changes in the context of the information or network society (Schiller 1996; Castells 1996; van Dijk, [1991] 2001, [1999] 2012). Equality and inclusion are important norms in any social and liberal democracy and in the perspective of equal global development. This perspective leads to the introduction of social, cultural and educational policies by governments and NGOs.

A third perspective is often ignored: the importance of the digital divide for security in society. However, as early as the first year in which the digital divide was discussed, an appeal was published for so-called universal access for all Americans to e-mail (Anderson et al. 1995). The argument was that those without e-mail access would become a security liability: the government should support e-mail access for all citizens not only to communicate with them but also to keep an eye on them. After more than twenty years of massive government and police surveillance of the Internet and other digital connections, this appeal now seems more urgent than ever. For example, a terrorist who uses only secret face-to-face conspiracy and old technologies such as bombs, trucks, knives and guns to kill people is a nightmare for the security organizations. This third perspective is now part of every security policy. Better a connection for all than no connection at all.

A brief history of the digital divide

The first-level divide: focus on physical access, 1995–2003

This brief history looks at the research or scholarly perspective of the digital divide and the societal perspective of media, politics and policy. Presumably, the *Los Angeles Times* journalists Webber and Harmon coined the term in their article of 29 July 1995 describing the social division between those who were involved in information technology and those who were not (Gunkel 2003: 501). A short time afterwards, the NTIA (part of the American Department of Commerce) popularized the term and supported it with census data, but at that time it used only the terms 'haves' and 'have nots'. The term spread both in the media and in American politics.

In 2001 the first, frequently cited scientific book about the digital divide appeared: Pippa Norris (2001) distinguished a *global* divide (industrialized and developing countries), a *social* divide (access of rich and poor individuals in each nation) and a *democratic* divide (those who do and those who do not use Internet resources for community engagement). Although her theory was much broader, she treated the concept of the digital divide primarily in terms of physical access, which means having a computer and an Internet connection. Norris framed the divide with reference to the diffusion of innovations theory. This theory, best known in the work of Everett Rogers ([1962] 2003), defines a number of groups who take up new technologies (innovators, early adopters, early and late majority people, and laggards) and the evolution of their endorsement in an S-curve.

This first phase of discourse and research was marked by a very rapid uptake of computer possession and Internet connections among the general population, first of all in the United States. Espousal was first by the innovators (the first 2.5 per cent) and the early adopters (from 13.5 per cent of the population), and then by the early majority (between 34 and 50 per cent). After 1993 the graphical interface of the World Wide Web considerably increased the popularity of the Internet. In 1995 less than 30 per cent of Americans owned a computer and less than 20 per cent a modem, while less than 10 per cent were permanently online among others using e-mail (NTIA 1998). However, in 2001 the figure was 56 per cent for computers and 50 per cent for the Internet (NTIA 2002) and several European countries had already passed the US in take-up (NTIA 2002).

Between 1995 and 2004 the gap in the adoption of computers and Internet connections between people with higher education, income or employment, the young, and those of the majority ethnicity in a country were increasing in comparison with people with low education, income or employment, seniors and ethnic minorities (van Dijk 2005). The first nationwide representative surveys to report this was one by Katz and Rice (2002), covering surveys from 1997 through 2001, and those published by the Pew Internet and American Life Project (Horrigan 2000; Lenhart 2000; Spooner and Rainie 2000).

In the second part of the 1990s the mood concerning the potential of the Internet and ICTs in general was very positive and optimistic. Approaching the millennium, even an Internet hype was observed. According to policymakers, every citizen, worker and consumer should have access to the opportunities of the Internet, and this seemed to be confirmed by the fast uptake. Soon critics pronounced that the digital divide was a myth (Brady 2000; Compaine 2001), non-existent (Thierer 2000) or rubbish (Crabtree 2001). The problem could be solved by the market offering ever cheaper and simpler computers and connections. Via the 'trickle-down principle', affluent first users would pay for cheaper products to be purchased later by users with lower income. Just as with other mass media, such as radio, television, video players and telephones, those in higher social classes would merely adopt computers and the Internet a bit earlier than others. American government agencies reached the conclusion that the digital divide was closing naturally. While the titles of the first reports of the NTIA contained references to people as 'have nots' and 'falling through the net', or were trying to define 'the digital divide' (NTIA 1995, 1998, 1999), around the election of George W. Bush as president the titles suddenly included words such as 'toward digital inclusion' (NTIA 2000) and 'a nation online' (NTIA 2002). At the start of the Bush administration all funds and initiatives supporting access created in the Clinton years were cancelled and the NTIA budget was severely cut. According to Hammond, the boss of the NTIA in 2000, the term 'digital divide' sounded too divisive. Instead, he preferred to talk about 'digital inclusion' (Rappoport et al. 2009). So, five years after its appearance, the digital divide was officially buried.

Yet, this was not the conclusion of scholarly debate and research into the digital divide; the number of publications reached a climax between the years 2000 and 2005 (Berrío Zapata and Sant'Ana 2015: 6). At that time research and debate were dominated by economists, telecommunications researchers and government or business policy-makers, almost exclusively American. The attitude of these researchers and policy-makers was technical and deterministic: the diffusion of this strong new technology, full of opportunities, was inevitable and would lead to near universal dissemination when market forces were enacted.

The second-level divide: focus on skills and usage, 2004 – present

In the following period, first scholars and then policy-makers moved beyond the parameter of physical access. Social scientists indeed first used such expressions as 'beyond the digital divide' (Mossberger et al. 2003), 'rethinking the digital divide' (Warschauer 2003), 'reconceptualizing the digital divide' (Selwyn 2004) and 'the digital divide as a complex and dynamic phenomenon' (van Dijk and Hacker 2003). Paul Attewell (2001) coined the terms 'first-' and 'second-level divide', the latter referring to computer use and literacy. A year later this term was made popular by Eszter Hargittai (2002), who primarily raised issues of unequal online skills. The core idea and critique of the shift was that having physical access was useless without the requisite skills, knowledge and support for effective use and that the digital divide problem was not first and foremost technological but social, economic, cultural and political (Selwyn 2004).

This period was marked by an even faster uptake of Internet connections and purchase of computers, which became smaller, faster and cheaper every year. While in 2004 less than 15 per cent of the world's population used the Internet, in 2014 that figure was already approaching 45 per cent (World Bank 2016). During this decade the early majority of the potential population in the developed countries using the Internet turned into a late majority, in some countries reaching the 90 per cent mark. The gap in computer and Internet access among people in the developed countries with different education, income, employment or social status, which had previously been widening (van Dijk 2005), was turned upside down. Now it was those with low education and income, together with seniors and females, who were adopting the technology faster than the others.

The popularity of the Internet grew considerably with the appearance of social media around the year 2004 and the arrival of mobile web access with powerful phones (3G), leading to a user experience that was altogether different. In the early 1990s the Internet was seen as a foreign and intimidating space that required technical expertise and digital competencies (Oggolder 2015). Now it became part of daily life for more than 70 per cent of the population in the developed countries. Using e-commerce, e-banking, e-government and social-networking sites became normal daily activities. In 2012 van Dijk and van Deursen (2014b) observed that, in the Netherlands, people with low education spent more leisure time on the Internet than those with higher education.

When, between 2010 and 2015, in a growing number of technologically advanced countries, home Internet access exceeded 90 per cent or more, often with broadband capacities, policy-makers in government and business tended to play down the problem of the digital divide. Simultaneously, faster connections and all kinds of terminals apparently made use of the Internet extremely easy: laptops, tablets, smartphones and touchscreens were everywhere. The digital divide was buried for the second time. The majority of people were using the web to find simple information and for messages, shopping, every kind of service and social networking. 'Even a two-year-old child can manage a tablet' was a popular expression at that time. In the US, only broadband diffusion was left as a problem for the government to solve, starting in the Obama years after 2008.

That the digital divide was dead was not the conclusion of most researchers and policy-makers pretending to have insight and a vision of the future. It was certainly not the conclusion of policy-makers and researchers at that time in the developing countries, where physical access and Internet use reached (far) less than 50 per cent of the population. In both developed and developing countries, many government and educational authorities realized that there was more than physical access to be considered. It became clearer that all those new users needed skills and useful applications to support the economy, society and culture. Unfortunately, policy directions to reinforce this were exploratory, occasional and not very effective (see chapter 9).

So it is not surprising that, following the fast adoption and popularization of the Internet, at least in the developed countries, the biggest concern for digital divide research became the skills of all those new users. The scope of research became considerably broader, to include the new issues of opportunity and inequality. The key term 'digital divide' was used less and less in publishing after 2004 (Berrío Zapata and Sant'Ana 2015). It seemed that between the early 2000s and 2009 the interest in such research was diminishing (Reisdorf et al. 2017: 108). In fact, the key words were changing, to 'Internet use', 'social media use', 'mobile use', 'digital or information literacy', 'digital skills or competencies', and others related to unequal opportunities and applications.

Between 2004 and 2012, new conceptual frameworks and operational definitions were created for digital literacy and typologies of Internet use or applications. Discussions started concerning what the differences might be between traditional and digital literacy and whether 'literacy' or 'skills and competencies' was the more appropriate term to use. Together with creating new conceptual frameworks, some researchers tested the literacies, skills or competencies in laboratories, field experiments and surveys (Hargittai 2002; Bunz 2004, 2009; van Deursen 2010).

The second issue of primary intention in this phase of digital divide research was Internet use and user groups. Several classifications were created, some based traditionally on general social-psychological gratifications or needs (Flanagin and Metzger 2001; LaRose and Eastin 2004), others on special Internet activities (Livingstone and Helsper 2007; Brandtzæg 2010; Kalmus et al. 2011; van Deursen and van Dijk 2014a, 2014b). These were studied in several wide-scale surveys of Internet use internationally.

A number of investigators observed that a *usage gap* was unfolding similar to the so-called knowledge gap that occurred in the 1970s with the mass media. This was seen as a gap between people using primarily information, education and career-oriented Internet applications and those using mainly entertainment and simple commercial and communication applications (Bonfadelli 2002; Madden 2003; van Dijk and Hacker 2003; van Deursen and van Dijk 2014a; Zillien and Hargittai 2009).

From 2004 onwards, most research was dedicated to differences and inequalities among computer and Internet users. Most popular were projects about the unequal use of a series of new media and applications perceived as hypes: blogs, chat or messaging boxes, social media, mobile phones and wearables. Studies were still predominantly American, though there were European scholars (mainly in the UK, the Netherlands and Spain). In Latin America, a number of Brazilian, Chilean and Mexican authors were active (see Berrío Zapata and Sant'Ana 2015 for the international distribution) while, in Asia, South Korea, Singapore and, more recently, China have been prominent in this research, showing that work in this area has become global.

The third-level divide: focus on outcomes, 2012 – present

While the focus of research on skills and usage continues today, in the last five years a new perspective has appeared. As the process of diffusion of computers and the Internet seems to be reaching saturation point, at least in the developed countries, some investigators and policy-makers wonder what its effect has been on people, organizations and societies. What are the outcomes (neutral) or benefits (normative) of computer and Internet access and use? Again, some individuals ask whether the digital divide has finally closed.

In 2010, José Robles Morales, Cristóbal Torres Albero and Óscar Molina coined the term 'third-level digital divide' (in Spanish). Two years later Robles and Torres Albero (2012) again suggested the term as a logical step after their survey of access and use of the Internet in Spain, although they did not account for outcomes in their study. They hypothesized that people without access and the necessary skills would not benefit from a growing number of online services that did not have offline equivalents, and they were afraid that digital inequality would reinforce classical social inequalities. In 2011, Wei and his colleagues from Singapore not only used the term but also demonstrated the third-level divide in a local experiment. They observed the effects of access (first level) and capabilities or skills (second level) on the self-efficacy and learning outcomes of 4,000 students.

Van Deursen and van Dijk demonstrated a much broader focus of outcomes or benefits of Internet use in two nationwide representative surveys in the Netherlands. The first was in the economic domain. In the spring of 2012 they reported on productivity loss among the Dutch workforce on account of a lack of digital skills (estimated at about 4 per cent of working time) and malfunctioning digital technology (another 4 per cent loss). See van Deursen and van Dijk (2014b). In the autumn of that year their representative survey of the Dutch population contained a long list of questions concerning the potential benefits of using the Internet on all domains, economic, social, political, cultural, educational and personal development. It showed that people with higher education and jobs and the young generations were benefiting much more from the Internet than those with low education or jobs and the elderly. Examples of such benefits were lower prices for products, greater chances of securing a job or finding a party to vote for, better education opportunities, more and better health information and treatment, opportunities to acquire new friends, and even more chance of forming romantic relationships (see van Deursen and van Dijk 2012). At that time only the positive outcomes of Internet use were taken into account.

In 2015, Helsper, van Deursen and Eynon published a comparison of British and Dutch survey data, called *Tangible Outcomes of Internet Use*, which observed and conceptualized Internet outcomes in four fields of resources: economic, cultural, social and individual well-being. Two years later Ragnedda (2017) offered a theory focusing on the third-level digital divide, dealing with the question of whether the outcomes simply extend traditional forms of inequality or whether they also include new forms of social exclusion.

In the last five years of this recent phase of research, there has been universal access to the Internet and their terminal devices in the most technologically advanced developed countries. The so-called laggards and the digitally excluded now comprise less than 10 per cent of the population, whereas in other developed countries this figure is 20 per cent to one-third of the population. However, in the developing countries it is variously between 50 and 90 per cent of the population – far from universal access (ITU 2017).

As, in the developed countries, all parts of the population are using the Internet daily and digital media in every activity – work education, leisure, social networking, commerce and services – the effects or outcomes of these activities register with both researchers and policy-makers. The positive and negative effects of Internet and digital media use are observed and discussed in all media. Policy-makers are no longer focusing only on physical access or digital skills and useful applications of the Internet. The 2016 World Bank *Digital Dividends* report is about the many, mostly positive, effects of Internet use in several domains of society. The outcomes of Internet use are also outlined in the *Inclusive Internet Index* of the Economist Intelligence Unit (2019). This policy think tank concludes that 'an inclusive Internet is not just accessible and affordable to all. It is also relevant to all, allowing usage that enables positive social and economic outcomes at individual and group level.' The indicators for assessing countries in this index were not only availability and affordability but also relevance and readiness to use the Internet.

The focus on outcomes of the third-level digital divide is also the main focus of this book. The emphasis in my earlier general book was the second-level digital divide, highlighting digital skills and inequalities of use (van Dijk 2005). The main questions I want to answer here are 1) does digital inequality or the digital divide reduce or reinforce existing, traditional inequalities?, and 2) does the digital divide create new, previously unknown, social inequalities? These questions will be highlighted in the last part of the book. In the first part I shall deal with the causes of the outcomes of Internet and digital media: motivation for or attitudes towards using digital media, physical conditions of access, digital skills and usage patterns.

Chapter overview

Chapter 2 is about the empirical investigations and the theories created concerning the digital divide in almost twenty-five years of research. Has the body of research grown or diminished in these years? Have there been times of rising and declining interest? Was the research primarily quantitative or qualitative? What were the main methods of data collection? Who were the most important subjects of research and which were the most important countries? Which were the most important empirical questions in the first-, second- and third-level phases of digital divide research? The second part of this chapter discusses the theories about the digital divide offered so far. What is the nature of these theories? Are they specifications of existing general theories or new theories focusing only on the digital divide? Have these theories been validated and tested in empirical research?

Chapters 3 to 6 are the core of this book. They describe and explain four phases of access or adoption of digital media: a) motivation or attitude towards gaining access, b) actually obtaining physical access, c) acquiring digital skills or literacy, and d) actual use of these media. These phases are in fact parts of my own theoretical framework proposed many years ago (van Dijk 2005), but they can still be used as neutral distinctions because they follow the focus of the three levels of digital divide research. I have no problem in describing different approaches than my own or research results of other investigators.

In chapter 3 the primary motivations for gaining access are discussed. In general, such motivations, and positive attitudes towards the use of digital technology, have increased considerably in the last twenty-five years. However, even when universal access is in sight in the most technologically advanced developed countries, motivations and attitudes remain important where unequal use is involved. Some people are much more motivated than others to purchase new hardware and software, to learn digital skills, and to use all kinds of Internet applications every day. We have in society not only have-nots but also want-nots. Who are they? This chapter contains mostly psychological research.

Chapter 4 summarizes the main research about physical access. This is the 'classical' and best-known part of digital divide research. It is primarily

economic, technological and sociological. Here familiar schemes of diffusion of innovation theory are examined, such as the adoption curves of
current and future users. What is the current situation of computer possession and Internet connection rates in developing and developed countries?
Does the physical access gap disappear when everybody has a computer and
an Internet connection?

In chapter 5 the discussion turns to research into digital skills or literacies. I will first list several conceptual frameworks invented for the study of
digital skills, competencies, literacies, so-called twenty-first-century skills
and others. Then I will list all the relevant causes and consequences of the
digital skills divide according to those frameworks. Who has the best skills
and to what level? Are the more highly educated and young people better
than others, as presumed in public opinion?

Chapter 6 is about divides in the use of the Internet and other digital media. The most important typologies of users and applications on
(mainly) the Internet will be enumerated. Concerning unequal use, we
look principally at the frequency and diversity of applications. We will see
that all known social differences in society are reflected in the use of the
Internet and other digital media. However, does this use only reflect or also
reinforce usage patterns? The knowledge gap thesis of the 1970s assumed
that the use of the traditional mass media leads to more information for
people with higher educational attainment and more entertainment experience for those with lower educational attainment. Is a similar gap also
growing on the Internet?

Chapter 7 is about the positive and negative outcomes of access and use
of the Internet and other digital media. Who benefits most from access and
usage: people with higher education and income, people in professional
jobs, young people in general? Or are all categories of the population benefiting equally? Who is better able to cope with such negative outcomes as
excessive use, cybercrime or abuse, and loss of security or privacy?

Chapter 8 concerns the relation between digital and social inequality.
This chapter contains the main messages of the book. Here again the principal question is whether digital inequality is merely a reflection of social
inequality or whether it might lead to more or less inequality in general.
The second question is whether the use of digital technology will reduce or
reinforce existing inequalities. When the Internet and other digital media
first appeared, people thought that inequality of information and media use
would be reduced. Once people obtained access and acquired a minimum
of usage skills, information would be relatively easy to find everywhere
(online) and at any time. The Internet was cheap or even free to use, as costs
were paid via advertising.

In the last twenty years this optimistic expectation began to fade. It was observed that social, economic and cultural inequality was rising in large parts of the world. The entire societal context is significant for the evolution of the digital divide. This chapter focuses, first, on the context of those other inequalities that existed before the advent of the Internet and, second, on new types of inequality in the context of the information society and the network society.

The final chapter of this book is about policy perspectives to solve the problem of the digital divide. But can the digital divide be closed completely, or can it only be mitigated? In this chapter several policy measures in all domains of society will be discussed that at least ameliorate the problem. They are listed with reference to the four phases of access discussed in chapters 3 to 6 along the main social domains: work, education, business, leisure, citizenship and culture. I will address both governments and the business world (producers, users and designers of digital technology), together with educators, politicians, community or civilian organizations and users themselves.

2 Research into and Theory of the Digital Divide

Introduction

In this chapter I will describe the characteristics of the research tradition concerning the digital divide over the last twenty years. There have been various approaches, so I will outline the general methodologies and theories, listing the most important research questions, themes, disciplines involved, strategies and methods, and, finally, the published results and their impact.

I will then go on to describe the theories formulated from four perspectives: the acceptance of technology perspective, the materialist perspective, the social-cultural perspective and the relational perspective. Deriving from these I propose a broad theoretical framework that can be used to explicate in the following chapters the results of research so far.

Research into the digital divide

Questions

At the turn of the twenty-first century the main question was *who* possessed a computer and an Internet connection and who did not. Researchers considered the primary demographics such as income, educational level, gender, ethnicity and employment status. The first institutions producing the statistics were national government departments and bureaus of official statistics, international bodies such as the United Nations, the World Bank and the European Commission (Eurostat), and telecom corporations with their branch organizations, such as the ITU. At the same time, scholars found the statistics produced by these bodies to be rather superficial. They wanted to know *why* particular people had computers and Internet connections and why others did not. To find answers their primary method was to conduct surveys, either on a large scale for whole countries or on a smaller scale for specific communities, such as students.

These scholars also asked what might be the development of access among populations in both rich and poor countries. Would everybody gain access to computers and the Internet as rapidly as had been the case with the television a generation before? Would there be only 5 or 10 per cent of the population in rich countries left without access, as for example with landline telephones, or would particular segments of the population lag behind permanently? Pippa Norris (2001) called the first projection *normalization* and the second *stratification*. To create these projections scholars used existing economic theories or those regarding social stratification and diffusion of innovation. One of the economic projections of normalization was the *trickle-down principle*, in which the adoption of new technologies always shifts from higher to lower social classes of income, education and occupation (Compaine 2001). Those who have the necessary resources first pay for the cost of a new technology, which makes adoption cheaper later on for those of lesser means.

However, others thought that the continuing stratification and cultural divisions among status, lifestyle and innovativeness were responsible for persisting inequalities of access. Finally there were the more technically oriented scholars who expected that digital media would become more and more easy to use, thus closing the access gap.

When physical access surged after 2000, another question arose: did those with access have sufficient skills to use digital media? In response, Eszter Hargittai (2002) announced the second-level digital divide, which focused on skills and usage. It was soon discovered that the skills needed were not only technical or operational but also information- or content-related. To investigate this, researchers began to use performance tests in laboratories and school classes. A subsequent question was whether people exhibiting inadequate digital skills were the same individuals as those with problems gaining physical access. Were differences of income, occupation, education, age, gender and ethnicity the same where both skills and access were concerned?

After 2005, questions about inequality of usage came to the fore. What was the frequency of use (time), the amount of use (number of applications) and the diversity of use (types of applications) among different social categories of users? Several Internet user typologies were created and a number of large-scale surveys were conducted to describe and analyse all these aspects.

Between 2012 and 2015 a growing number of researchers asked what were the benefits of having and using the Internet and what were the real disadvantages of not being online. Examples of benefits were cheaper products and services, the possibility of finding a job, maintaining and increasing social contacts, chancing on a partner, searching for information and help with health problems, examining political information, signing up for an educational course and following a cultural activity. The potential negative

Table 2.1. The main research questions concerning the digital divide

Issue	Question
Possession	Who has computers, the Internet and other digital media?
Motivation	Who wants computers, the Internet and other digital media?
Evolution	What is the growth in access to digital media in developed and developing countries?
Skills	Who shows sufficient digital skills?
Usage	What are the frequency of use, the amount of use and the diversity in use among all social categories of users?
Benefits and disadvantages	What are the benefits of being online and what are the disadvantages of not being online?

outcomes – excessive use, unwanted, unsafe and even criminal behaviour, and loss of privacy and the quality of face-to-face communication – were not examined. Researchers observed that the negative effects meant that some people didn't use the Internet, but there was no particular focus on this (see table 2.1).

Themes and disciplines

During the years of the first- and second-level digital divide, particular research themes became important. According to a systematic analysis of the literature between 1997 and 2012 by Berrío Zapata and Sant'Ana (2015), the seven themes shown in table 2.2 were the most popular. Top of the list was *access for consumers* – to know who has access to digital media and networks and why; this was seen from both a supplier and a consumer perspective.

The second most popular theme was *development*, in the context of the level of development of a country and the innovativeness of its society. The

Table 2.2. The top seven research themes into the digital divide

	Research theme
1	Access for consumers
2	Development and innovativeness of countries
3	Education
4	Empowerment: community-building and participation in society
5	e-Health
6	e-Government and e-Participation
7	Capacities and applications of digital technology

Source: Berrío Zapata and Sant'Ana (2015).

enormous gap of physical access between developed and developing countries was a major topic of research, alongside the assumed boost given to development by gaining access to and the use of digital technology.

A third important theme was *education,* primarily the teaching of the necessary skills and competencies and the integration of ICTs in schools and universities.

In fourth place was *empowerment,* which could mean either the power of digital media for community-building and self-organization or the increase in active participation in several domains of society through digital media.

The fifth theme was *e-health,* particularly where the unequal use of health applications was concerned. It was assumed to be literally vital that people should have the skills to make use of such applications.

Issues of *e-government and e-participation* formed the sixth most popular topic. Inequality of access and the use of online public and social services, information about citizen benefits and the sources of information to participate politically were the points of investigation.

The last theme consisted of the *capacities and applications of digital technology,* which involved the differences in access, skills and usage entailed by particular versions of digital media. Often discussed were the differences between narrowband and broadband access, the opportunities of mobile technology for general use, and the evolution of the computer from mainframes and PCs to laptops, tablets and smartphones.

According to Berrío Zapata and Sant'Ana's summary (2015: 12), 'the main areas of research are education, administration, development communication, telecom and IT, medical sciences, information science and economy.' The question is whether these disciplines have investigated the digital divide.

The disciplines dominating the first-level digital divide were *economics,* primarily the consumer economy, together with *telecoms and IT.* The main researchers were the authors of the NTIA reports and the ITU reports, as well as individual authors such as Compaine (2001) and the marketing scholars Hoffman et al. (2000).

An early *political scientist* investigating the digital divide was Norris (2001). She was followed by *education scientists* such as Warschauer (2003), Solomon et al. (2003) and Selwyn et al. (2006); Warschauer also introduced the field into development studies by focusing on the digital divide in developing countries.

Sociologists and *media and communication scholars* showed an interest at the time the second-level divide was introduced. American scholars such as Servon (2002), Mossberger et al. (2003), DiMaggio et al. (2004) and Witte and Mannon (2010), Europeans such as Mansell (2002), van Dijk (2005),

Zillien (2006), Livingstone and Helsper (2007) Robles and Molina (2007) and van Deursen (2010), and the South Korean Park (2002) combined sociology and media or communication science.

Currently, digital divide research is an interdisciplinary activity, with scholars scarcely making a distinction between economic, social, political, cultural, psychological, technical and information or communication science. Similarly, this book aims to be fully interdisciplinary in describing and explaining the digital divide.

Strategies and methods

Which strategies and methods of research have been used to ask all these questions? The most general strategy is making a choice between *basic* and *applied research*. Although the digital divide is clearly a societal problem, so far most research has been fairly basic, describing the current state of affairs. Only a small minority of projects investigate solutions applicable in practical settings. It seems that both scholars and policy-makers want first to understand the development of the digital divide before trying to find solutions.

The second characteristic of digital divide research is that it is more *descriptive* than explanatory. As I will argue in the rest of this chapter, it lacks a fully fledged theory. Much of it contains correlations between access, skills or use and personal demographics of age, gender and ethnicity or socio-economic factors such as income, occupation and education (Scheerder et al. 2017; van Laar et al. 2017). The deeper social, economic, cultural and psychological causes of the correlations are seldom addressed.

Digital divide research also is overwhelmingly *quantitative*. Most of it is based on data collected from large-scale surveys and attempts to capture the wider picture. Although this produces vast amounts of information, it does not come up with the precise mechanisms explaining the adoption and use of the technology concerned in everyday life. Qualitative ethnographic or field research is relatively sparse; examples are by Stanley (2003), Wyatt et al. (2005), Katz (2006), Ito et al. (2009), Clark (2009), Loos (2012) and Correa (2014). The dominant demographic and socio-economic variables in survey research lead more to socio-*economic* than to socio-*cultural or psychological* determinants of Internet use (van Dijk 2006; Scheerder et al. 2017).

By far the most frequently used *strategy* in digital divide research is the survey and the resulting official statistics, which are used for all phases: motivation, physical access, skills, usage and outcomes. Nationwide representative surveys, the predominant type, are most often in the form of self-administered questionnaires. Experiments are a second common strategy, mostly used for registering usage patterns and outcomes in particular situations in the field; they can also, for example, provide different connections, devices and support for comparison. The third strategy is performance tests administered by educational institutions or by scholars investigating digital skills. These are mainly used to observe skills or levels of literacy, although surveys are employed most for this purpose. The least frequently used strategy is ethnography or research observing actual, daily use in restricted fields.

So, the methods of *data collection* in digital divide research are primarily questionnaires that lead to scientific reports or official public statistics. Direct observation of behaviour is seldom practised except for in performance tests. Longitudinal research is scarce so it is difficult to show trends such as the evolution of phases of the digital divide. International comparisons made by international institutions such as the UN, the ITU, the World Bank, the EU and the World Internet Project, combining reports of universities in more than thirty-five countries (www.worldinternetproject.com), are more frequent.

Data analysis comes mainly from descriptive data. For major data sets, correlations or at best regressions are most popular. Causal modelling of big data sets is not frequent because of the lack of a comprehensive digital divide theory (see the second part of this chapter). Comparisons mostly involve only two models with a combination of a few variables.

Publications and their impact

Wang et al. (2011) mapped the 'intellectual structure' of the digital divide research community between 2000 and 2009 with a bibliographical and social-network analysis of 852 scientific journal papers and their 26,966 citations. They concluded that 'the digital divide has gained the reputation as a legitimate academic field, with digital divide specific journals gaining the status required for an independent research field' (2011: 54). A broader bibliographical and network analysis, including books, theses, conference and working papers and policy documents from 1997 through 2015, found 102,000 key terms in the text and 5,970 in the titles of English-language publications (Berrío Zapata and Sant'Ana, 2015). Spanish publications showed 13,400 key terms in the text and 672 in the titles and Portuguese publications 486 in the text and four in the titles. Other languages were not covered.

This brings us to an important observation. More than half of the scientific publications and their citations of research into the digital divide come from the US, followed by the UK and other European countries. In the Spanish-language sphere, Spain, Mexico and Chile have most publications and citations, while in Portuguese it is Brazil (Berrío Zapata and Sant'Ana, 2015). Other languages and countries are not covered, but they comprise a small minority in the scholarly domain. This means that the majority of research originates in English-speaking developed and (relatively) rich countries. Policy-oriented publications issued by (inter)national institutions (the ITU, the UN, the World Bank and others) focus on both developed and developing countries.

Another striking observation is that there is a divide between the academic publication domain and the policy-oriented domain of (inter)national institutions and official public statistics. The academics tend to cite each other, as do the policy researchers, meaning that the policy impact of academic research is possibly less than that of policy research and official statistics about computer and Internet access or use. This issue will be discussed in the final chapter.

Digital divide research is publicized much more in journal articles, conference and working papers and reports than in books. Nevertheless, books receive relatively higher rates when it comes to citations (Berrío Zapata and Sant'Ana 2015: 7). Most articles are publicized by the English journals *First Monday* (open access), *New Media & Society*, *Information Society*, *Information, Communication & Society*, *Telematics and Informatics* and *Telecommunication Policy*. The most important authorities in the first decade of the twenty-first century were Pippa Norris, Mark Warschauer, Eszter Hargittai, Jan van Dijk and Donna Hoffman (see Berrío Zapata and Sant'Ana 2015: 8, 10).

Theories concerning the digital divide

The current status of theories

It was claimed above that digital divide research is predominately descriptive and that it has not yet produced a fully-fledged theory. However, many people have attempted to provide a theory, some of whom are developing fresh ideas and others are adopting or adapting existing theories. A fully-fledged theory requires at least four elements (see table 2.3).

Current and past research has produced many empirical statements and

Table 2.3. The four elements of a scientific theory and their characteristics

Element	Characteristic
Theoretical statements	A coherent number of statements or axioms containing basic concepts and their relationships, perhaps to be portrayed in a model, which provide the so-called hard core of a theory
Basic concepts and operational definitions	Concepts with definitions for empirical research
Empirical statements	Statements that have been tested and supported in empirical investigations
Heuristics or preferred method	A method of research appropriate to the statements

operational definitions of concepts used for mostly descriptive and correlational research. However, coherent theoretical statements or axioms and causal analysis are frequently lacking. Even when causal analysis is used, for example with structural-equational modelling, the model is not a reflection or a test of a basic theory explaining phenomena related to the digital divide. Most often they are merely an assembly of factors or variables which are statistically related and *seem to* follow a logical causal path.

We are looking for systematic theories containing both theoretical and empirical statements and heuristics or empirical methods to test them in the future. Presently we have only a number of *perspectives of developing or adopting theories*. I will now discuss four perspectives.

The acceptance of technology perspective

Currently, a series of so-called acceptance of technology principles is available for a theory which might explain many aspects of the digital divide. Most theories of technology acceptance are psychological, drawing on behaviour, attitudes, motives, expectancies and intentions. Behavioural intention is the most important factor in such psychological theories.

The oldest theory in this domain is the *theory of planned behaviour* (Ajzen 1991; Ajzen and Fishbein 2005). This is a rationalist theory describing the ways in which people consciously choose or reject a particular technology. The initial causes are threefold, relating to behavioural, normative and control beliefs. Some people have a positive attitude towards computers, mobile phones and the Internet and others have negative attitudes towards them. In the following chapter I will show that these attitudes are very important in adopting or rejecting digital media. Normative beliefs here are stimulated (or not) by people's social environment to become part of the digital world. Clearly this holds for the present young generation – 'the digital natives' – who have grown up with digital media. Finally, the perceptions of people that they are able to apply digital media, for example by means of skills, are the control beliefs. These three beliefs come into play before people accept a technology. So behavioural intention is treated here as a dependent variable.

A second theory frequently used to explain the intention to use a new technology is called the *technology acceptance model* (Davis 1989). In this theory the perceived usefulness and ease of use are what initially determine the attitude towards a new technology. These are in fact the attributes of a particular technology as perceived by potential users. In the history of digital media they have become ever more important in closing the digital divide. Generally, in the last twenty-five years both the usefulness and the ease of use of computer and Internet applications have dramatically increased. However, these measures remain different for different parts of the population.

The third psychological theory of technology acceptance is the *unified theory of acceptance and use of technology* (Venkatesh et al. 2003). This theory claims to combine all statistically significant factors of technology acceptance for individuals in the context of organizations. Here the expectancies of the effort needed and the performance of the technology concerned, together with the influence people perceive from their social environment, are decisive for the intention to use it.

Probably the most popular technology acceptance theory in digital divide research is the *diffusion of innovations theory* (Rogers [1962] 2003). The psychological backbone of this broad interdisciplinary theory is the process involved in the decision to adopt or reject a new technology. The focus and dependent variable here is not the behavioural intention to adopt, as in the former theories, but adoption itself. This entails both personal characteristics, such as innovativeness, and societal factors, such as social norms for change, and the decision process is informed by communication sources. People are persuaded by the perceived technical characteristics of the innovation concerned. Digital media might be accepted when it is seen that they have a relative advantage over other or older media, when they are compatible with familiar media, when they are not very complex to use, or when people are able to observe and experiment with them in their own environment.

These four theories focus only on the first phases of access to a new technology, while the following theories concentrate on the use of a technology (see figure 2.1). The first is the *uses and gratifications theory* (Rosengren

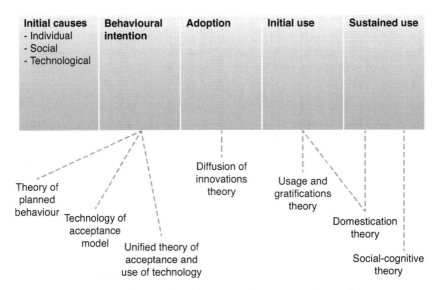

Figure 2.1. Acceptance of technology theories in their various phases of acceptance

et al. 1985). The core of this theory of media and communication science is the sequence of basic needs, motives and gratifications searched for and obtained in using particular media. Some researchers, for example, list various gratifications gained through using the Internet (Cho et al. 2003; Song et al. 2004; Stafford at al. 2004; LaRose and Eastin 2004). Users seeking these gratifications are motivated to gain access and develop the corresponding skills.

The sociological and communication theory known as *domestication theory* (Silverstone and Hirsch 1992; Silverstone and Haddon 1996) focuses on the initial and continued use of media in everyday life. The ethnographic method used here is to observe how people (re)design available media to suit their own context and their own purposes.

The last acceptance theory here is *social cognitive theory* (Bandura 1991, 2001). This is a theory of social learning, as people observe the media use of others in order to inform their own learning. After a while their expectations of the results are raised and they develop habitual use (LaRose and Eastin 2004 combine this theory with the uses and gratifications theory).

The materialist perspective

The materialist perspective looks primarily at the economic *means* and the social *opportunities* people have to acquire digital media. Previously in this chapter we have seen that socio-economic demographics form the most important variable in digital divide research. Income, socio-economic status, occupation, job and level of education have here been framed in more abstract categories emerging from existing social and economic theories.

Consumer economic theory attempts to explain the digital divide of (mainly) physical access through market costs. When prices drop – for instance, as chips, batteries and screens become cheaper – consumers are more able to purchase the relevant hardware. When new digital media first emerged, purchases were made largely by people with substantial incomes, while those on low incomes waited for prices to go down. This mechanism is called the 'trickle down principle' (Compaine 2001; see chapter 1).

From the perspective of Marxian economics, however, the digital divide would still exist because people's living conditions and access to digital media are determined by more than market costs. One of the most popular theories from the materialist perspective is the *capital theory* of Bourdieu (1986), whose types of capital have been a source of inspiration for digital divide researchers in constructing variables for surveys. *Economic capital* – money, property and other assets – is exemplified by questions about income and the possession of connections, devices, software and subscriptions. *Social capital* – social relationships and network connections – is identified by questions about social support in gaining access, learning skills and using digital media. *Cultural capital* is acquired in three forms: embodied (learning knowledge and language), objectified (obtaining cultural goods) and institutionalized (diplomas, credentials and professional qualifications). It is seen in digital divide surveys in questions about the educational level attained by respondents and the status acquired by using digital media.

However, in digital divide research the variables identifying these types of capital are usually used only descriptively by finding correlations between kinds of access and these variables. The background of Bourdieu's theory of social stratification, distinction, status and power in society (Bourdieu and Passeron 1990) is rarely discussed.

The second theory in this materialist perspective is the *structuration theory* of Giddens (1984), which states that social structures are made by human action via their rules and resources. Social and cultural rules constrain actions and several kinds of resources make them possible. In digital divide research, a set of resources is assumed to be supporting access in all phases. The most important are material resources (income and property), mental resources (knowledge and social or technical skills), social resources (connections and relationships) and temporal resources (time to spend in any activity, including using digital media). Social and cultural rules point to the way in which people are supposed to employ digital media.

Similar to Bourdieu's capital theory, Giddens's structuration theory is mostly used by digital divide researchers to derive lists of resources and rules in order to correlate them with access.

The socio-cultural perspective

The socio-cultural perspective shows more interest in the *meaning, significa-tion and (re)construction* of the use of and access to digital technology. The point of departure is that access to and the use of digital media are embed-ded in everyday life and the socio-cultural context. The domestication theory mentioned earlier also belongs to this perspective. Researchers writ-ing from this perspective are active in sociology, anthropology and media studies.

One of the pioneers is the classical sociologist Max Weber ([1922] 1978). Some digital divide researchers have recently called attention to a Weberian approach (Ragnedda and Muschert 2013; Blank and Groselj 2014; Regnedda 2017). While Weber was also an economist, he did not think that inequality was determined only by economic factors; factors such as status and prestige were important too. His argument starts with (un)equal *life chances*, comparable to the materialist concepts of resources and capital. Through these chances people *conduct their life* (in this context, they use digital media in their own way in everyday life). In so doing they have a number of *life choices*. The result is a particu-lar *lifestyle* – here in which digital media have more or less importance. These four aspects of life in the work of Weber are explained by Regnedda (2017: 70).

Lifestyles determined by a particular possession and use of digital media create prestige and status; people with the same lifestyle create status groups of which many people wish to be a part. For young people, mobile phones and wearable computers form an important lifestyle and status marker. Without these symbols they are likely to be excluded socially. However, it is not only age that leads to cultural distinctions in the digital divide. Cultural differences of gender, ethnicity, social class, jobs or professions, and knowl-edge of languages can lead to unequal access and use of digital media.

We have seen that socio-cultural factors have been neglected in earlier digital divide research. Nevertheless, this perspective is useful for all phases of access, not least in the phase of motivation and the cultural distinctions of digital media usage.

The relational perspective

The last perspective to be discussed is a particular methodological approach which might possibly lead to a new basic paradigm. Most digital divide research is undertaken on the basis of so-called methodological individualism (Wellman and Berkowitz 1988). It often deals with individuals and their characteristics – level of income and education, employment, age, sex, and ethnicity. This is the usual approach in survey research, which measures the properties and attitudes of individual respondents.

A different perspective is the relational or network approach (Wellman and Berkowitz 1988; Monge and Contractor 2003). Here the most important units of analysis are not individuals per se but the relationships between individuals. Inequality is not just a matter of individual attributes but also one of categorical distinctions between groups of people. This is the view of the American sociologist Charles Tilly: 'The central argument runs like this: Large, significant inequalities in advantages among human beings correspond mainly to categorical differences such as black/white, male/female, citizen/foreigner, or Muslim/Jew rather than to individual differences in attributes, propensities, or performances' (Tilly 1998: 7). Other important categorical distinctions are employers and (un)employed, management and executives, people with high and low levels of education, the elderly and the young, and parents and children, while at the macro-level we may observe the categorical inequality of developed and developing countries, sometimes referred to as the core and periphery. The first of these pairings is generally the dominant category as far as the possession and control of digital media is concerned; the exceptions are the last two mentioned above – the elderly and parents.

The dominant category is the first to adopt the new technology, thus gaining an advantage to increase power in its relationship vis-à-vis the subordinate category. The example of gender inequality is instructive:

> Gender differences in the appropriation of technology start very early in life. Little boys are the first to pick up technical toys and devices, passing the little girls, most often their sisters and small female neighbours or friends. These girls leave the operation to the boys, perhaps at first because the girls are less secure in handling them. Here a long process of continual reinforcement starts in which the girls 'never' learn to operate the devices and the boys improve. This progresses into adulthood, where males are able to appropriate the great majority of technical and strategically important jobs and, in practice, keep females out of these jobs. (van Dijk 2005: 11–12)

Table 2.4. Theoretical perspectives on the digital divide

Perspective	Focus or core
Acceptance of technology	Attitudes, motivations, expectancies, intentions, adoptions
Materialist	Capital and resources
Socio-cultural	Meanings, life chances, life choices and lifestyles
Relational	Relations and power

An advantage of the relational perspective is that it reveals the concrete mechanisms of growing inequality as compared to the more superficial explanations found among individual attributes (e.g. that females are supposed to be less technical). The perspective is also useful in the context of the rise of the network society, where interactions become ever more important (van Dijk [1999] 2012). However, unfortunately the relational perspective is not yet much utilized in digital divide research.

A general framework for understanding the digital divide

With these different perspectives (see table 2.4) it is not easy to find a neutral framework for understanding the digital divide. Any such framework will have to be derived from a very broad theory combining these four perspectives. With some hesitance I wish to propose my own theory for this task. It combines four of these perspectives, and it is open enough to allow for interpretation of almost every factor or variable of digital divide research (see figure 2.2).

The *resources and appropriation theory* (van Dijk 2005) is first of all a theory of technology acceptance, which it understands as a process – appropriation – rather than as a single intention or decision. This process is

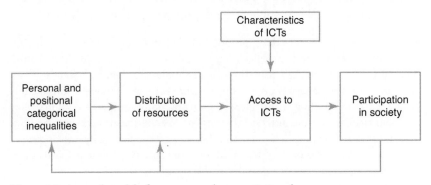

Figure 2.2. A causal model of resources and appropriation theory

behavioural: first people have to be motivated, then they have to acquire or purchase the technology, and, finally, they have to learn to use it by developing the relevant skills. This process follows the first and second level of the history of digital divide research.

This theory has its origins in the materialist perspective on account of the resources and personal and positional characteristics of individuals. In fact the theory conforms to structuration theory (Giddens 1984), since its core is a continual interplay of structures (rules and resources) and people's actions or behaviours. Resources are not only material but also mental, social and cultural, so the socio-cultural perspective of meaning has a place in this theory too. Finally, the relational perspective is relevant because of the personal and positional characteristics of the categorical pairs.

The backbone of the theory is presented in figure 2.2. Personal and positional inequalities lead to different amounts of resources. These resources determine the process of technology appropriation in four phases of ICT access (motivation, physical access, skills and usage), and the outcomes of this process lead to more or less participation in society in several domains (economic, political, cultural, etc.). ICT access also depends on the technical characteristics of the digital media concerned.

The hard core of this theory can be summarized as follows.

1   Categorical inequalities in society produce an unequal distribution of resources.
2   An unequal distribution of resources causes unequal access to digital technologies.
3   Unequal access to digital technologies also depends on the characteristics of these technologies.
4   Unequal access to digital technologies brings about unequal outcomes of participation in society.
5   Unequal participation in society reinforces categorical inequalities and unequal distribution of resources.

In this book the term '*access*' in statements 2, 3 and 4 is a sequence of four phases: motivation/attitude, physical access, digital skills and usage. This is a *linear* logic in the model as a whole. In fact the model can also be applied in a *circular* manner. For example, motivation and attitude also influence skills and usage, and more usage often leads to more motivation.

The following *personal categorical inequalities* are often observed in digital divide research:

• age (young/old)
• gender (male/female)

- ethnicity (majority/minority)
- intelligence (high/low)
- personality (extrovert/introvert; self-confident/not self-confident)
- health (abled/disabled).

The same goes for the following *positional categorical inequalities*, which operate on both a personal and a societal level:

- labour position (entrepreneurs/workers; management/employees; employed/unemployed)
- education (high/low)
- household (family/individual)
- network (core/peripheral)
- nation/region (developed/developing; urban/rural).

In most empirical observations the first of these relational pairings have more access to digital technology than the second.

The following *resources* frequently figure in digital divide research, sometimes under other labels, such as economic, social and cultural capital:

- temporal (time to use digital media)
- material (income and property)
- mental (cognitive capacities and technical abilities)
- social (a social network to assist in acquiring and using digital media)
- cultural (lifestyle, status markers and habits in using digital media).

These factors are summarized in the full empirical model of this theory presented in figure 2.3. The theory was tested in several nationwide surveys in the Netherlands and the UK between 2010 and 2015 and, using the statistical method of *sequential-equation modelling*, was found to fit the data in causal path analysis (see van Deursen and van Dijk 2015b; van Deursen et al. 2017; van Deursen and van Dijk 2019).

This model will be used as a general framework and source of inspiration for understanding the results of digital divide research in the remainder of the book. However, the following five chapters will also review approaches and results of research other than those of the author.

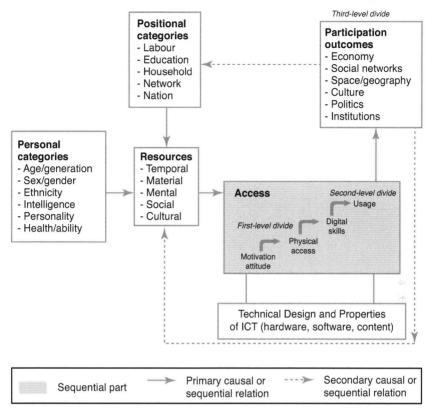

Figure 2.3. A causal and sequential model of digital media access

3   Motivation and Attitude

Introduction: who wants digital media and feels fine about them?

The nature of the first stage of access to and adoption of digital media is psychological. Human needs, motives, attitudes, expectancies, gratifications and intentions drive the decision to purchase a computer or other digital medium and to connect to a network such as the Internet. The following stages are also driven primarily by the general motivation to engage (or not) with the digital world. Without sufficient motivation and a positive attitude, individuals will not develop digital skills or competencies. Similarly, they will not use digital media very often – only perhaps for one or two purposes. Finally, the outcomes of digital media use will be disappointing for those with low motivation and a negative attitude.

The following section deals with basic concepts. There is an abundance of psychological concepts in the literature concerning motivation. How are these related to each other? What are the most important needs, motives, gratifications, attitudes and expectancies to use or, indeed, not to use digital technology?

The third section is about the *causes* of different motivation. These are not only personal (age, gender, personality and the like) but also positional, partly societal characteristics. Those in gainful employment and students might well have more motivation to use digital technology than the unemployed. Those who are part of a social network where everybody uses digital media are also likely to be motivated. People living in developed and technologically advanced countries are assumed to be more motivated than people in developing, less technologically advanced countries. People with these personal and positional characteristics have resources that partly determine motivation and attitude for access and for use. These resources are not only of a mental kind. They might also be material, social, cultural and temporal resources.

The next section discusses the *consequences* of motivation and attitudes. Since different people purchase different quantities of hardware, software and services, they will develop different levels of digital skills, and the frequency and variety of their use of digital media will be different. Finally, the benefits they attain will be different. So, the digital divide will become wider with a lack of motivation in all phases of access.

The final section will describe the *evolution* of the level of motivation and attitudes towards digital technology. In the 1980s, even in the developed, technologically advanced countries, the majority of the population was apprehensive about the advent of the digital age. When the use of computers, the Internet and mobile telephony spread in the 1990s, motivation and positive attitudes increased considerably. Currently, close to 90 per cent of the population in the developed countries are motivated to use computers and the Internet (van Deursen and van Dijk 2012; van Deursen 2018). Even people in their eighties want to learn to use computers and the Internet, if only to e-mail and chat with their grandchildren. Nevertheless, we observe that computer anxiety and technophobia remain even in developed high-tech countries and that the motivation of those in developing countries is still lagging behind. See the emphasis on the perceived lack of relevance of digital applications in these countries (ITU 2017; Economist Intelligence Unit 2019). Evolution also means that the range between people who are complete non-users of the Internet, at one end of the spectrum, those who are low-frequency users, and those, at the other end, who are high-frequency users, online for perhaps more than twelve hours a day, is becoming wider in every part of the world.

Basic concepts

People's reasons for use and non-use of digital media expressed in surveys can be conceptualized differently in psychological terms. Positive reasons can be framed in intentions (before) and gratifications (after) using specific applications. Negative reasons are mostly given by non-users and ex-users and are of a more general kind. The reasons for non-use listed in table 3.1 can be understood as explicit needs, motives, attitudes or expectations, though they may hide some implicit reasons. Someone who says that they don't want a computer or smartphone might not genuinely like such tools, but it may be that they are not able to afford them or do not know how to work them.

The negative reasons found in surveys and listed in an average order of frequency in table 3.1 have remained much the same over the years. In rich countries the affordability explanation may have declined over time, but it still exists. Rejection of digital media was high in the 1980s and lower at the time of the Internet hype around the millennium. However, it recently began to increase again when many negative uses of the Internet and social

Table 3.1. Reasons for the non-use of computers and the Internet over time

Order of importance	Reason
1	I do not want it (not interested).
2	I do not need it (not useful).
3	I reject the medium (cybercrime, Internet addiction, unreliable information, poor communication and others).
4	I have no computer or Internet connection.
5	I do not know how to use it; it is too complicated.
6	It is too expensive.
7	I have no time/I am too busy.

Source: Summary of many international surveys.

media were reported. The most surprising thing is that the reasons for rejecting digital media are the same today as they were fifteen years ago; compare the lists of surveys in several countries in van Dijk (2005: 29–30), Reisdorf and Groselj (2017), Helsper and Reisdorf (2017), World Bank (2016) and Digital Inclusion Research Group (2017).

The distinction between the basic psychological concepts of needs, motivations, gratifications, attitudes and expectancies is insufficiently made in digital divide research. Figure 3.1 shows the series of psychological factors behind media behaviour. The first concepts or factors in this model derive from uses and gratification theory (see chapter 2). *Needs* are basic drives, motivations are conscious intentions, and gratifications come from satisfying rational and emotional goals. Needs are requirements for survival.

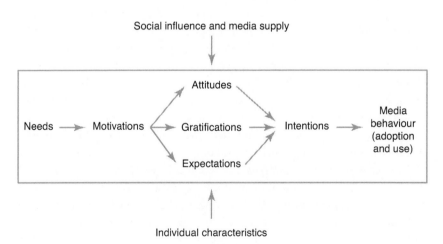

Figure 3.1. A sequential model of psychological factors behind media behaviour

Maslow (1943), for example, lists basic needs ranging from physical needs (food, water and sex) and safety to those of love/belonging, esteem and self-actualization. While digital media cannot at present be said to fall into the category of basic needs, in the future almost every job might require ICTs and online dating may become dominant. Currently, it is primarily the 'higher' needs of identity, communication, sociality and status that are met by the use of digital media.

While needs can be partly unconscious, the *motivations* derived from these needs are always conscious. A single reason to act might be a motive, and motivation often involves several motives. For example, the use of social media and online gaming might be motivated by such reasons as socializing, learning, the wish for personal development, or just passing time.

Gratifications are the desired results of a goal-oriented act – the fulfilment of one or more motives. When the goal is reached and also creates a positive emotion, such as pleasure, it will be repeated. When goals are not reached and negative emotions occur, gratifications will no longer be sought.

In the literature we find many lists of needs, motivations and gratifications for the adoption and use of digital media. For example, in the perspective of uses and gratification theory, Katz et al. (1973) identified the needs of traditional media; Cho et al. (2003) transformed these for digital media. Papacharissi and Rubin (2000) enumerated the motivations and Sundar and Limperos (2013) and Dhir et al. (2016) list gratifications for specific new media. These are summarized in table 3.2. The right-hand column of

Table 3.2. Needs, motives and gratifications in seeking and using digital media/the Internet

Needs	Motives	Gratifications
Material/practical	Managing daily life	– Coordination – Utility/shop – Convenience
Cognitive	Learning	– Information seeking – Novelty/news
Affective	Feeling	– Excitement/arousal – Self-assurance
Personal	Personal development	– Identity creation – Status gain
Social	Socializing	– Social connection – Social interaction – Finding other opinions
Escape/play	Passing time	– Entertainment – Gaming – Consuming

the table gives a number of gratifications that are recognized as important goals, especially of using the Internet, while the other two columns give the background needs and motives of these goals. (Gratifications are not concrete applications such as using social-networking sites, which are discussed in chapter 6, 'Usage'.)

Needs, motives and gratifications are not the only psychological factors affecting intentions to adopt and use digital media (see figure 3.1.). The theory of planned behaviour and the technology acceptance model focus on perceptions and attitudes. *Attitudes* may be cognitive (knowledge about digital media), emotional (experiences or feelings) or normative (judgements). They may also be general (liking or not liking technology) or specific (liking or not liking a particular technology/medium). General attitudes vary from technophilia and computer mania to technophobia and computer anxiety (see below). Specific attitudes may be positive or negative. For example, at the time of the Internet hype around the year 2000, positive attitudes were dominant. Fifteen years later the downsides of Internet use became evident. Negative attitudes towards digital media are one of the most important causes for non-use and ex-use (van Dijk 2005; Reisdorf and Groselj 2017; Helsper and Reisdorf 2017).

Expectations are the hopes that using digital media will have particular outcomes and are based on knowledge and perhaps past experience of using these media. These are the basic concepts of social cognitive theory, discussed in chapter 2, which focuses on the experience and habits of people who have already used such media for some time. LaRose and Eastin (2004: 370) observed the following six expected outcomes of Internet use. With *novel* outcomes, people expect to find information or news. In *activity* outcomes they assume that they will be entertained – for example, by playing games. The third expectation is to find *monetary* outcomes – searching out cheap or free products and services or saving time by e-shopping. The fourth expectation contains *self-reactive* outcomes: these are benefits for the self, such as passing the time, relieving boredom or feeling less alone. The fifth expectation is gaining *status*: an individual might find others respect them because they are using the Internet. The final expectation is finding *social* outcomes, such as coming across friends and love partners or obtaining support from others. Following the rise of social media since 2004, the expectation of social outcomes has become the most important.

Intentions are mental states determining whether people wish to act or not. This is the last step before accepting and adopting or rejecting a technology (see figure 3.1). This decision can be blocked by external factors, for instance facilitating conditions. Someone who clearly wants to purchase a computer or find an Internet connection can be prevented from doing so because they have no money, while someone else might not want a computer and Internet connection but is obliged to accept and use them because their job or course of study requires them to do so.

Causes of differences in motivation

Having defined the basic general concepts of motivation and attitude concerning digital media, we are now looking for their causes. We will use the model shown in figure 2.3 (see p. 33), which is broad enough to contain all the relevant causes found in the literature. We will start with the resources important for the first stage of access (motivation and attitude), followed by the particular personal and positional categories of individuals.

Resources and motivation

Among the five resources to be discussed (temporal, material, mental, social and cultural), the first three – temporal, material and mental – are primary, while the other two – social and cultural – come to the fore when digital technology is fully incorporated in society.

To be motivated to use digital media, people must first have *the time* to do so. Positive conditions are having a job or being engaged in a course of a study in which you have to use technology for several hours a day; thus workers or students are motivated whether or not they actually like digital media. People with much free leisure time might also have motivation. To our surprise, we found in a nationwide survey in the Netherlands in 2011 that the unemployed and those unable to work were the most frequent Internet users (van Deursen and van Dijk 2014b), taking advantage of it for passing time, entertainment or finding a job.

Negative conditions arise of course when people are busy with other activities, such as housework or childcare, being engaged in manual labour, or being involved in sports. On the other hand, digital media in daily life may lead to an increase in positive stimuli and attitudes and a decrease in negative ones. The result may be that an excessive use of smartphones, computer games and Internet activities dominates and harms other activities and needs, such as sleeping, regular eating, face-to-face communication and physical exercise.

The second conditional resources are *material* and consist of income, property and appliances for the household, work or study. When people have fewer of these material resources, or simply cannot afford them, they will be less motivated towards their use. This is a major aspect in poor countries. However, in rich countries there is a substantial proportion of the population that can afford perhaps only one device and connection, while the wealthy may have access to several types of computers and connections.

Mental resources are *capacities* such as intelligence, technical ability and literacy rather than characteristics of motivation or attitude. People who have these capacities will be much more inclined to use digital technology. While intelligence is partly hereditary, technical ability and literacy are learned and improved in practice. People who are good at numbers, fluent in reading and writing and tech-savvy are much more motivated to use digital media than those who are illiterate, who cannot calculate and who lack the ability to use complicated devices.

Related to technical ability, people who lack self-confidence or who have neurotic personalities (see below) may show *computer anxiety* (Brosnan 1998; Chua et al. 1999; van Dijk 2005). This is a feeling of discomfort, stress or fear experienced when confronting computers, though it can also be caused by frustration arising from bad experiences. Another phenomenon is *technophobia* – fear of technology driven by a particular negative attitude or opinion. It is a rejection of the world of computers and a distrust about their positive outcomes. Today such fears are also about privacy and security, a loss of freedom through government control or corporate tracking and when confronted with disinformation.

The fourth type of conditional resources are *social*. Social relations and networks are crucial in learning and to support and motivate people to use digital media or to develop a positive attitude towards them. People with a wide social network are more likely to look for access to digital media than those who are isolated socially (van Deursen et al. 2014; Courtois and Verdegem 2016). For young people, relations with peers are the first trigger to gaining access to and mastering digital applications; the alternative is to become socially excluded. There is a certain status in, for example, uploading a video to YouTube or owning the latest new device or app, and this is extremely motivating in particular for the young. For older people, the social context and support of friends, family, colleagues and neighbours also is vital for motivation: in particular they participate in social media in order to communicate with family, friends and (grand) children.

Finally we come to *cultural* resources – cultural capital or goods as well as such properties as status and esteem. In the developed countries people live in a material environment of computerized workplaces and homes full of devices and screens and generally have a positive attitude towards using digital media. In developing countries such technology is often limited to universities, schools, hospitals, government departments, workplaces, libraries and Internet cafés, so people do not routinely come into contact with it.

Positional categories and motivation

There are five positional categories, the first of which is the *labour* position. The unemployed, people unable to work and many pensioners will have fewer resources and less motivation to use digital media, and perhaps negative attitudes as well. Those who are part of the workforce may have jobs that require computer skills, and so many unemployed people looking for a job have the motivation to learn such skills. However, all research indicates that individuals in higher occupations are the most motivated and in general have the most positive attitudes.

Similarly, twenty-five years of research have shown that people with higher *education* have both more resources and greater motivation and positive attitudes where using information and communication technology is concerned. The information aspect of digital media is particularly attractive for such individuals (van Dijk 2005, 2013), while the communication aspect is popular among all levels of society.

Being part of a family *household* also indicates a probability of being motivated to use digital media. In every country, households with the highest rate of computer possession and Internet access are those with school-age children. Single-person households have the lowest rates, especially among those with low levels of education. Larger families increase the efficiency and reduce the individual cost of using devices and connections.

Being part of a *social network* is also very relevant for the motivation and attitudes towards using digital media. The network helps in developing skills and locating attractive applications such as social media and phone apps. Being in a central position in a wide network is also more beneficial than being in an isolated or marginal position.

The last positional category is being an inhabitant of a particular *nation or region*. The average motivation and positive attitude among residents of rich and technologically advanced countries and for people in urban areas is obviously much stronger, as advanced countries and urban regions offer all the necessary infrastructure not only to motivate but also to use digital media. This is rarely the case in less advanced countries. For example, a university professor in Burundi has less chance of being motivated and less necessity to use digital media than a professor in Sweden.

Personal categories and motivation

The first personal category is *age* or generation. All research in this area shows that young people are more motivated and positively oriented towards digital media use than seniors. Young people are more inclined than older people to accept every new technology, but today's young people have grown up with digital technology – they are digital natives. They cannot imagine a world without digital media, and it helps shape their identity. People over the age of forty, on the other hand, have had to adapt to the new technology, but when they manage to do so it may well become part of their everyday lives.

The second category is *gender*. Males were the first to be motivated to adopt digital technology, but females were quick to catch up, and in developed countries gender differences are becoming smaller and smaller. However, in countries with strong patriarchal cultures, both rich and poor, there remains a gender gap in motivation.

The third category is *ethnicity*. This is a sensitive category because it is often combined with race. In fact the differences in motivation and attitude among specific ethnic, migrant or native, majority or minority groups in a country are related more to economic deprivation, discrimination and cultural preferences than to race. Minority and migrant groups actually use digital media as tools to communicate with their home communities and for support in difficult situations. A survey in the United States showed that Asian Americans have the highest motivation to use digital media, more than Anglo-Americans and much more than African and Hispanic Americans (Perrin and Duggan 2015). However, this was related not to race but to socio-economic status and cultural or online preferences.

One of the reasons why the highly educated are more motivated to use digital media is their assumed *cognitive intelligence*. This is related not only to the individual's level of education but also to the nature of information and communication technology, which addresses the capacity to process information. A related personal category is the level of *literacy*. Computer software requires a high level of literacy, so people who have a low level of literacy will have less motivation. The latter tend to use digital media for pictures, videos and music. In developing countries a large proportion of the population is illiterate, and even in developed countries perhaps 10 to 30 per cent is functionally illiterate. Such people have to rely on remembering which key strokes to use.

Another personal category often related to motivation to use digital media is *personality*. The evidence here is inconclusive (Russo and Amnå

2016). The influence of personality depends on the particular applications and technologies used. In the literature, the 'Big Five' dimensions of personality (openness to experience, extroversion, conscientiousness, agreeableness and neuroticism) are linked to computer and Internet use with applications such as social media. People having the trait of openness to experience (curiosity, appreciation of news and new ideas) like to explore the web (Tuten and Bosnjak 2001) and to find new and old relationships via social media (Correa et al. 2010).

Extroversion (assertiveness, sociability, liveliness and having positive emotions) used to be negatively related to Internet use because the web was assumed to be impersonal, while introverts liked the advantage of being able to protect their anonymity (Hamburger and Ben-Artzi 2000). However, it was found that extroverts were drawn to social media for its sociability and potential for expression (Ryan and Xenos 2011).

Conscientiousness (being organized, structured, reliable and dutiful) was observed to be positively related to the use of a computer because of its routine and reliable operations (Finn and Korukonda 2004). However, the Internet environment, especially the chaotic settings of social-networking sites, was found to be too unstructured for conscientious people (Landers and Lounsbury 2006). Agreeableness (being kind, considerate, likeable, prosocial and helpful towards others) was also negatively related to Internet use (ibid.), since such individuals prefer face-to-face communication. However, this might change with the development of social media.

Finally, neuroticism (feeling anxious, nervous and insecure) has been linked with computer anxiety (Hudiberg 1999; Chua et al. 1999) and the unsafe environment of the Internet (Tuten and Bosnjak 2001). Those with neurotic personalities have found more positive experiences in the relatively safe setting of social networks among existing friends (Correa et al. 2010).

The last personal category to be discussed is *health or ability*. It might be thought that disabled people would be highly motivated to use digital media to compensate for a handicap, especially if they have a mobility problem. However, their position in fact means that many disabled people are less motivated: on average only half of the disabled people in the world are in the workforce, and many are isolated socially (OECD 2010; WHO 2011). Other problems are that interfacing aids for the disabled are underdeveloped and that many organizations do not follow official web guidelines of accessibility for such individuals (Velleman 2018).

The causal argument is summarized in figure 3.2. The order of elements in the categories follows my own estimations observed from survey results.

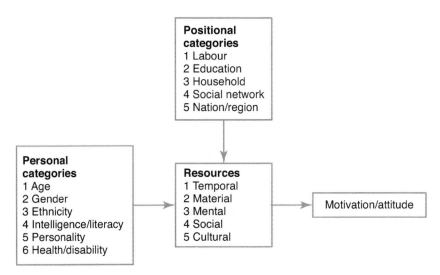

Figure 3.2. Causal model of differences in motivation and attitude for access

The consequences of differences in motivation

Effects in other phases of digital media access

There are consequences for all subsequent phases in the process of acceptance of this technology of having more or less motivation to use digital media and having either positive or negative attitudes towards them (see the test of the model in figure 2.2 in van Deursen and van Dijk 2015b). The first is the decision to access the Internet: people have to weigh the cost of the purchase of a computer against the cost of everything else they need to buy. Less motivation and a negative attitude will also lead to less practice in developing advanced operational and content-related digital skills (see chapter 5). However, the biggest effect may be observed in the phase of usage (ibid.). Increasing motivation and maintaining positive attitudes lead to more frequency and variation of use in particular applications. People with high motivation tend to become frequent users of apps. The final consequence is whether or not people take advantage of the benefits of digital media (van Deursen et al. 2017). The higher the motivation, the more benefits, although negative effects may arise when too much use results in addiction and other excessive behaviour.

Table 3.3. Spectrum of Internet users: from non-users to frequent users, 2017

Non-users	Ex-users	Low users	Regular users	Frequent users
		0–4 hours a week	4.1–24 hours a week	≥ 24.1 hours a week

Shifts in the spectrum of Internet users

The level and change of motivation and attitudes towards digital media causes shifts in the spectrum of Internet users. This spectrum comprises at least five categories of Internet use (see table 3.3).

The motivations and attitudes of *non-users* were discussed at the beginning of this chapter (see table 3.1, p. 36). Lack of motivation and negative attitudes are major causes of non-use, especially in rich countries. Next to the have-nots we find the want-nots. *Ex-users* are the 'dropouts' of the Internet, temporary or permanent. About fifteen years ago in the US they formed perhaps 10 per cent of (former) Internet users (Katz and Rice 2002; Lenhart et al. 2003). Today, this figure may be less than 5 per cent. For example, in the UK in 2013 it was 3.5 per cent (Reisdorf and Groselj 2017). However, in poor and developing countries the figure may be higher. Structural causes of dropping out are becoming unemployed, getting divorced and becoming homeless, while individual causes include a growing negative attitude towards and dislike of the Internet or computers.

Low users in 2017 are people using the Internet for up to 4 hours a week and for relatively few online activities. In the UK in 2013 they accounted for 21 per cent of the population, while non-users comprised 18.1 per cent (Reisdorf and Groselj 2017). Low users generally have negative attitudes towards technologies and the Internet in general (ibid.: 1172). For those in the developed countries, motivation and attitude factors are probably more important than the usual demographics of deprivation mentioned in the literature (education, job, income, gender, age and social network). *Regular users* in 2017 are estimated to be online for 4.1 to 24 hours a week. In the developed countries this category accommodates the biggest proportion of the population. *Frequent users* today – the digital information elite of society – engage in Internet use for more than 24 hours each week. On average they are extremely motivated to use digital media, and they also enjoy the greatest benefits, as well as suffering from high workloads and excessive Internet use.

The evolution of motivation and attitudes

Three epochal shifts are occurring in the level and nature of motivation and attitudes towards the use of digital media. The most important is that positive motivations and attitudes are growing in the general population following the diffusion of digital media in society. Non-users become low users and low users tend to become regular or frequent users. In the 1980s and 1990s, when traditional media held sway, motivations to use digital media were low and attitudes were marked by negativity. Even in 2002 more than half of American and European non-users (roughly half of the population) declared in surveys that they did not plan to use the Internet (Lenhart et al. 2003; Katz and Rice 2002; Van Dijk 2005). But soon afterwards the mood changed and, increasingly, larger numbers of people were inspired to go online.

Today, I think it likely that more than 90 per cent of the populations of technologically advanced countries now make use of the Internet (see for instance the Dutch surveys of van Deursen and van Dijk 2012 and van Deursen 2018). It is becoming increasingly necessary to have access in order to function as a member of society in these countries. The populations in developing countries are probably still lagging behind. However, positive and negative attitudes are mixed worldwide because of the appearance of the detrimental effects of Internet use (see chapter 7).

The second shift in the level and nature of motivation and attitude is that the gaps between the various positions on the spectrum probably become wider. The *frequency of use and amount of activity* between non-users, ex-users and low users, at the one end, and regular and frequent users, at the other, is growing. While the latter develop greater motivation and more positive attitudes, non-users and low users remain at the same level.

The related third shift is that those on the right-hand side of the spectrum *benefit* more and more from the use of the digital media (see chapter 7), resulting in a feedback loop of greater motivation and more positive attitudes.

4 Physical Access

Introduction: who possesses digital media?

At the time when research was taking place into the first-level digital divide (1995–2003), physical access was the main focus of scholars, policy-makers and public opinion. Today a common misconception is that the problem of the digital divide has been solved because almost everybody in the developed world is assumed to have some kind of computer, smartphone and Internet connection. In this book I argue that the problem *only starts* when everybody has a computer, smartphone or Internet connection! This is why my previous book was called *The Deepening Divide* (2005). Here I will show that this deepening divide tends to lead to more digital and social inequality, and I will make suggestions as to how to prevent this or at least to ameliorate it. This does not mean that the lack of physical access is no longer a problem. On the contrary, physical access is a prerequisite for reaching the next phases: developing digital skills, properly using computers or the Internet, and benefiting from them. In this chapter I show that the problem of physical access is here to stay, not only in the developing countries but also in the developed countries with very wide access. To demonstrate this, the concept of physical access has to be refined and specified.

In the following section the basic concepts concerning the types of physical access will be defined. A vast number of computer devices or applications and types of Internet connections have arrived in the last twenty years, which makes the problem of physical access more complicated. It is not only a quantitative problem but also a problem of quality: the nature and capacity of the technologies concerned.

In the third section, we will look first at the causes of not having physical access. What are the resources shaping physical access? What are the positional categories such as work and education and the personal categories such as age and gender? A fourth set of background factors has to be added here, which consists of the technical designs and characteristics of the vast number of types of digital media now on offer. The price, the complexity, the user-friendliness and usability of all these types also affect physical access.

This will be followed by a discussion of the consequences of more or less physical access. What are the concerns of not having physical access? In which way will it affect the following phases of skills, usage and outcomes? What will be the diffusion of digital media in society as compared to traditional media and what will be the result? Will everybody acquire physical access to digital media in the future, or will part of the population be excluded permanently?

The last section deals with the evolution of the digital divide vis-à-vis physical access. What is the historical pattern observed? Did the division in physical access start with a growing gap among populations and countries? Did this gap close at all? What will be the future: will there perhaps be other gaps following the arrival of various new types of digital media?

Basic concepts

In this book, as in previous ones (van Dijk 2005; van Dijk and van Deursen 2014), I want to make a distinction between three concepts: physical access, material access and conditional access. My definition of *physical access* is *the opportunity to use digital media by obtaining them privately in homes or publicly in collective settings* (schools, libraries, community centres, Internet cafés and other places). The first option is private ownership and the second is collective use. In the history of diffusion of digital media in society, physical access was at first largely collective, and this remains the case in developing countries. Today, however, there has been a shift from collective to individual adoption in the use of mobile computing with smartphones. This is also the case in developing countries, where mobile phones are increasingly displacing the need to go to a centre such as an Internet café. Currently, the collective setting needed for mobile computing is to be within reach of some kind of Wifi. However, powerful or advanced computers and broadband connections are still needed for work and education in collective settings and for leisure applications requiring a high capacity in private settings.

The second concept, *material access*, is broader than physical access. It can be defined as *all means needed to maintain the use of digital media over time, including subscriptions, peripheral equipment, electricity, software and print necessities* (e.g. ink and paper). In an even broader definition, it also includes the expenses of elementary *computer courses* required to be able to use digital media, additional expenses which tend to increase over time as software changes and which may eventually exceed the cost of the devices and connections.

The third, more limited concept is *conditional access*. Devices and connections are often not enough to acquire a particular service. Every Internet user is familiar with the numerous user names and passwords needed to get access to websites. Conditional access can be defined as *the provisory entry to particular applications, programs or contents of computers and networks. The conditions are payment or a particular position, membership or allowance* that is required at the workplace or schools and for membership of organizations or activities. Payment and entitlements are becoming increasingly important in the commercial and insecure World Wide Web.

All three types of access defined here are becoming more and more complicated when we look at the expansion of the types of devices and applications and network connections available today. Digital divide researchers and (non-)governmental organizations still focus on simple individual and country figures revealing the number of computer, mobile phone and Internet users per population. More researchers now break down such figures to include the type of computer (PC, laptop, tablet, etc.) and mobile phone (smartphone or feature phone), as well as whether narrowband or broadband connections are used, but there are few statistics of this kind and even fewer concerning the newest digital media and their capacities – equipment linked to the Internet of Things, devices of augmented reality such as smart glasses, virtual reality headsets and wearables (watches and activity trackers). The focus of research needs to shift from measuring separate digital media to taking into account the processing and communicating capacities of the total information system or networks linking separate devices. This means having an eye for *the quality and capacity* of all digital media connected in a system.

Hilbert et al. (2010) and Hilbert (2016) criticised the simple and stand-alone traditional approach and instead measured the amounts of information processed and transmitted by digital media and networks. These measurements are of the information-processing capacity of countries and individual installations, with the value of bits that each piece of equipment can store, the amount of kilobits per second (Kbps) it can communicate and the amount of MCps (million computations per second) it can compute (Hilbert et al. 2010: 168, table 2). This might appear to be a rather technical approach. Still, most users know that a broadband connection is much faster than a narrowband connection, that a smartphone gives a much better performance than a feature phone, and that a desktop or laptop computer can accomplish more than a tablet.

In this chapter I will try to take into account both this diversity and the technical quality and capacity of digital media.

Causes of divides in physical access

Resources and physical access

The immediate differences observed in physical, material and conditional access are due to people's resources. Evidently, *material resources* are by far the most important. Almost all research shows that income is most relevant for gaining access to digital media. Although basic digital media have become cheaper in the last thirty years, many people around the world, including those of modest means in rich countries, still cannot afford them.

Clearly, income is strongly related to employment or occupation and the level of education attained. Surveys often show that it has an independent effect (Zhang 2013; Bauer 2017). The wealthy have a good number of the best computer devices and phones, broadband Internet at home and mobile access via smartphones, and expensive and extended subscriptions. Those of modest means may own only one type of computer and one phone, lack home broadband, and perhaps have only a cheap feature phone and a basic subscription.

The second important resources are *social*. People enjoying many social relationships benefit from support, perhaps in acquiring a second-hand or borrowed computer, together with all kinds of software, peripherals and appliances and the use of an Internet connection at the home of others. Such relationships are vital in getting access to the world of digital media, especially in developing countries. Unfortunately, many poor people have fewer social relationships than rich people, and their social isolation can amplify digital exclusion.

In this book I often claim that social and *cultural* causes are just as relevant to the digital divide as economic causes. Cultural resources are ideas and values solidified or materialized in habitual behavioural patterns, cultural distinctions and artefacts. The most important of these are observable status markers, lifestyles, and how people react to the social world around them. Flashy new media devices are status markers for many, and some tech-savvies immediately want to attain distinction by having the latest gadget. They part with large amounts of money to purchase such items. Others may have lifestyles marked by spending all day using several kinds of digital media. This applies particularly to those living in the colder countries of the northern hemisphere, who pass more time indoors, while those in the sunnier southern countries are accustomed to living a more outdoors life. Finally, those involved in using digital media all day for entertainment purposes require more hardware, software and high-quality Internet access than those who use digital media occasionally for information and communication tasks (Robinson 2009).

Compared to material, social and cultural resources, temporal and mental resources are less important for physical access. People who do not have the time to use digital media might still possess them, and mental resources, while crucial for motivation, have no direct influence on physical access. A notable exception, though, are individuals with serious mental and physical handicaps, who actually seldom purchase digital media.

Positional categories and physical access

Work and education are the principal factors driving the distribution of material, social and cultural resources. In the 1990s, those with office jobs and in management positions were the first to obtain computers, though, while academics, teachers and technicians actually used them themselves, managers and directors tended to delegate computer work to their secretaries. At that point manual and unskilled workers were unlikely to have access to computers, while using both computers and the Internet became a necessity in administrative and commercial jobs in most middle-class occupations.

Today, it remains the case that, in almost every national survey undertaken in the developed countries, people in such occupations have more access to computers and the Internet than manual and unskilled workers. Although the gap has closed since the 1990s, those employed in middle-class jobs tend to have 100 per cent access while those in the lower occupations have approximately 70 to 80 per cent access. For example, Arabs in the state of Israel, who generally have lower incomes and less education, hold primarily manual and unskilled jobs and so have less access (Mesch and Talmud 2011). In the developing countries overall, the gap between the employed and the unemployed and between the well-educated and those of low education is still very pronounced (World Bank 2016; ITU 2017).

The second positional category is *education*, which is closely related to the category of labour but also has an independent effect. Individuals in education simply need a computer and Internet connection, at least in developing countries. In the 1990s the gap in use between those with high and low education was very wide, though it began to close about 2005. For example, in the US in 2000, the gap in physical access between people with at least a college degree and those with high school education or less was 59 percentage points (Perrin and Duggan 2015). In 2015, 95 per cent of people with college education or a graduate degree said they were Internet users, while the figure for those who had not completed high school was 66 per cent.

In the developing countries the gap is still growing today (World Bank 2016; ITU 2017), with the uneducated lagging considerably behind those who have completed schooling. In the future the gap will close here too, but most likely it will persist to a larger extent than in the developed countries.

The third positional category determining physical access is being an inhabitant of a particular *nation*, together with living in an urban versus a rural or a rich versus a poor *region*. Despite the fact that some individuals may have plenty of personal resources, they also depend on the economic and technological infrastructure and wealth of their country or region. There are differences in the reliability of the electricity supply, technological support after frequent breakdowns, the availability and reach of public access points, the economic support of governments and businesses with their subsidies or prices, and the educational support of schools.

The divides between developing and developed countries have always been wide, and in the 1990s and between 2000 and 2010 they were only becoming wider (see figure 4.1). Since 2010, Internet access has been growing at the same speed in all countries, so that after 2020 the gap will become

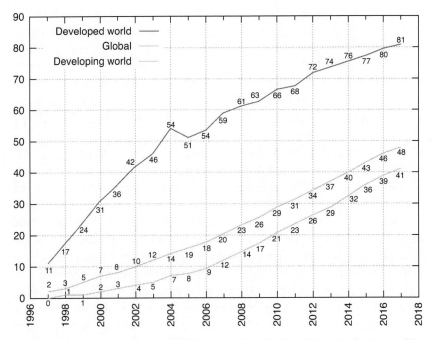

Figure 4.1. Internet users per 100 inhabitants in the developed and developing world

narrower. A saturation phase is approaching in many developed countries, and the proportion of those online in the developing countries is nearing 50 per cent.

However, access in the developing countries is not growing at the same speed in middle-income and low-income countries. In the middle-income countries, among whom are the new emerging markets in East Asia, South Asia and South America, access is growing fast, while the poorest countries are lagging behind, with figures of less than 10 per cent (Zhang 2013: 522; Hilbert 2016; ITU 2017: 13).

In every country, urban regions have much more physical access than rural regions. Remote places often have less reach and broadband capacity. The countryside offers less work and fewer schools requiring information and communication technology than cities, with their schools of higher education, government departments, and financial and industrial concerns. Poor inner-city districts, however, have less access than affluent suburban neighbourhoods.

The fourth positional category is living in a particular *household*. On average, single-person households have less access to computers and the Internet than multiple-person households, especially families with school-age children. These benefit from a single connection and are able to share computers, other devices and subscriptions.

The last positional category is having a particular position in a *social network*. Networking allows new ideas and practices to spread (Valente 1996), and a central role in a large network enables individuals to find and share the best hardware, software and applications. People who are socially isolated offline and gain only a marginal place in a social network online find less support and fewer opportunities (Tilly 1998).

Personal categories and physical access

The most frequent personal categories affecting physical access observed in research are age, gender and ethnicity/race. Rarely noted is the category of (dis)ability. Intelligence and personality have influence on motivation and attitude but no direct effect on physical access.

By far the most important personal category is *age*. In all countries young people have more and earlier access to computers, mobile phones and Internet connections than older people. This is both a generational and a structural effect. *Generational effects* are the strongest, since individuals over the age of forty did not learn to use the digital media in their youth and have to learn to use them at work or by themselves at home. Those born after

1980 (the Millennium generation) have grown up with and been educated with digital media. As this generation ages, a shift will take place: middle-aged people and the youngest generation will tend to have equal access to and use of digital media.

However, at the same time *structural effects* are at work. Digital media have become so vital for society that the elderly are catching up. In the developed countries a majority of people over sixty-five now have computers, smartphones and Internet connections and also use social media and other Internet applications.

A negative structural effect in terms of equal access among older people is also evident. Young people are naturally more innovative and want to experiment with digital media, while seniors are more attached to traditional media. Another structural effect is that young people are required to follow modern educational systems, while older people have to learn to use digital media via adult education computer classes. Structural effects tend to remain, while generational effects will disappear after a couple of generations.

The balance of the generational and structural effects today is that the gap in physical access between the young and the old continues to be pronounced. It is not as wide as it was twenty years ago, but in both developed and developing countries it is still noticeable. For example, in the US in 2015, only 58 per cent of people aged over sixty-five had Internet access, while people between eighteen and twenty-nine had 98 per cent access and those between thirty and forty-nine had 93 per cent. Worldwide, the young between the ages of fifteen and twenty-four had 71 per cent Internet access in 2017, while those older than twenty-five had only 48 per cent. However, in the developing countries the distribution was larger (67.3 versus 40.3 per cent) than that in the developed world (94.3 versus 81.0 per cent; see ITU 2017).

The second important category is gender. In terms of physical access, the gender gap between women and men is much smaller than the age gap. In 2017, it was 11.6 per cent worldwide (ITU 2017). In developing countries, people have less access at home, and many women, if employed, are only in manual or unskilled jobs. The result is that the gender gap in the developing countries is much wider than that in the developed world. In 2017 it was 16.1 per cent on average (25.3 per cent in Africa) as compared to the average of 2.6 per cent in the developed world. The Americas even reveal more access for females than males – +2.6 per cent! (see ITU 2017: 19).

The third important personal category is *ethnicity*, though in the domain of the digital divide this category pertains mostly to economic and educational disadvantage, social isolation, or spatially concentrated poverty and cultural preferences. The only independent effect of ethnicity consists of particular cultural preferences in wanting or using particular digital media.

In multi-ethnic countries such as the United States and Brazil, gaps in Internet access between the ethnicities are significant but not as wide as we have seen with age. In the US, English-speaking Asian Americans had the highest figure of access in 2015, at 97 per cent, while white Americans had 85 per cent, Hispanics 81 per cent and African Americans 78 per cent (Perrin and Duggan 2015). In Brazil, whites had significantly more Internet access than non-whites between 2005 and 2013, while access to a mobile phone was not significant; divides in age, income and education were more important (Nishijima et al. 2017).

The last personal category affecting physical access is *(dis)ability*. Although the disabled could find many advantages from Internet use, especially those with mobility problems, they in fact have less physical access to and use of digital media. In all parts of the world this gap is significant (Fox 2011; Ofcom 2015; Duplaga 2017). Here again, disadvantages of low income, less education and unemployment are responsible, but there is an independent effect of disability too. In this case, the design of hardware and the web is to blame. Many devices are not adapted for people with physical handicaps, and official web guidelines for the blind and deaf are often ignored.

Technical characteristics

While digital divide research has primarily used simple and basic indicators of physical access, such as the percentage of computer and mobile phone possession and Internet access, after the year 2000 these indicators became less and less adequate to determine the distinction between inclusion in and exclusion from the digital world. Digital technology is changing very fast, and at least four characteristics require differentiation.

The first is the *technical capacity* of devices, software and connections. The range of power in the various devices is enormous, software is available in basic and extended versions, and Internet connection speed ranges from very limited narrowband through to super high-speed broadband. The quality of digital technology defines its potential use. Martin Hilbert (2016) argues that the gap in Internet access between the developed and developing countries is in fact much wider when compared with basic access, and that the digital divide in physical access is here to stay. He measured the installed bandwidth potential of 172 countries between 1986 and 2014 and found that the inequality between developed and developing countries is extremely high and concentrated in Asia (including Russia), with more than 50 per cent.

The second characteristic is *diversity*. Digital media have multiplied since 2000, and we now have a growing number of types of computer, from mainframes and PCs through laptops and tablets to smartphones with big or small screens. Software is available from very advanced versions to very simple apps. Internet connections are focusing on the web, fixed and mobile phones, television and radio, and the Internet of Things. The crucial fact here is that some people have all of these devices, together with their software, while others have at best only one, meaning that the inequality of technical potential is growing (van Deursen and van Dijk 2019).

Along with this growing diversity we see that *replacement* of basic devices and connections is taking place. The most striking trend is the transition to mobile devices and connections. The developing world went mobile from the start because fixed connections were too expensive. In the developed countries today, a shift is occurring from home broadband to smart mobile phones (Perrin and Duggan 2015). Similarly, people are exchanging PCs for laptops, tablets and smartphones. However, the importance for the digital divide is that these replacements do not necessarily have the same use potential. Feature mobile phones, laptops, tablets and even smartphones have less advanced applications and contextual convenience and offer less enjoyment to the user than powerful PCs with their big screens and broadband connections. The main advantages are in their mobility and price.

A fourth technical characteristic of digital media is that they are unstable, regularly break down, often have to be repaired, and continually require updates. This is the problem of *technology maintenance* (Graham and Thrift 2007; Gonzales 2014, 2016). In developing countries there are frequent electricity blackouts and often a lack of transport for people to reach places such as Internet cafés; it can be difficult and expensive to repair broken mobile phones and old PCs. Figure 4.2 shows the causal argument so far (the order of factors in the boxes, apart from that for technical characteristics, is estimated).

The consequences of divides in physical access

Divides in physical access are a necessary condition of all the subsequent phases arising from the adoption of digital media: skills, usage and outcomes. The early assumption was that, once everybody had access to a computer and the Internet, the digital divide would be over.

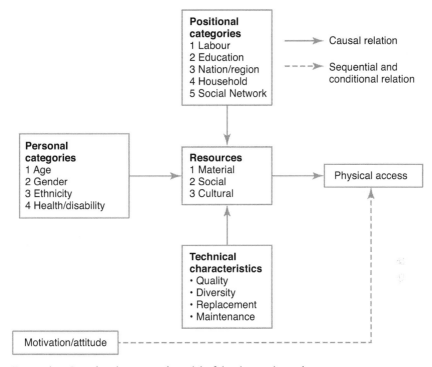

Figure 4.2. Causal and sequential model of divides in physical access

Physical, material and conditional access leads to the opportunity to learn *digital skills*. However, the quality of the hardware, software and connection available, and the time they are accessible to a user if they are sharing them in the context of public access, also affect the opportunity of obtaining digital skills.

Physical, material and conditional access affects *usage* too. Quality and time determine the type and frequency of digital media use. A broadband Internet connection that is constantly live stimulates much more daily use and high-quality application than a narrow-band dial-up connection. An advanced high-capacity PC offers more usage opportunities than a tablet. A smartphone makes a world of difference compared to a simple feature phone.

Finally, the *outcomes* of unequal use of disposable hardware, software and connections can be quite different. Someone who possesses high-quality examples of all available technical resources will benefit more than someone who has only one inferior device, a slow connection and a basic Internet subscription.

The evolution in divides of physical access

While the common perception, based on theories of market economics and the diffusion of innovations, is that the physical access divide will eventually close, I call this into question.

The principal market economic theory is the trickle-down mechanism, whereby status products that are first adopted by the rich or the elite later become affordable for the less well-off. The mechanism was first applied to the digital divide by Thierer (2000) and Compaine (2001), who stated that the digital divide was a myth and that it would soon disappear. The market would solve the problem once cheaper and simple computer products appeared. It was just that people with lower incomes would only gain access later, as was the case with previous media innovations – the telephone, the radio, the television and the video recorder.

Computer products and connections are indeed much cheaper than before and in the developed countries are now within reach of even relatively poor people. However, the digital divide of physical access has not disappeared because the technology constantly requires more, and more complex, investment than did radio, television and the telephone.

Diffusion of innovations theory, based on sociology, communication science, marketing and development theory (Rogers [1962] 2003), describes with the aid of the so-called S-curve the evolution of physical access or adoption of new media by various groups: the innovators (2.5 per cent), the early adopters (13.5 per cent), the early majority (34 per cent), the late majority (34 per cent) and the laggards (16 per cent). This model might be attractive for marketing scholars, but I have many problems with it (see van Dijk 2005: 62–5), as it is too deterministic (why should every medium reach 100 per cent of the population?) and normative (think only in terms of the names of the adoption groups: the first are good and the last are bad).

To 'save' the model of the S-curve, several qualifications are required. One is to define different groups of adopters. Pippa Norris (2001) distinguished two patterns in terms of the S-curve: normalization and stratification. In the *normalization* pattern, groups are only earlier or later in starting on the curve and faster or slower in following it; eventually all of them will reach the same goal of universal access. In the *stratification* pattern, groups from particular social strata (in terms of status, income and power) follow a different path on the curve. These groups have different resources at the start, so that the higher strata reach their peak earlier than the lower strata, who may never reach universal access (Norris 2001; van Dijk 2005).

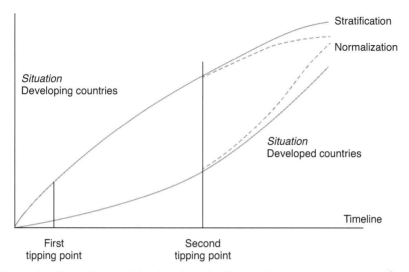

Figure 4.3. The evolution of the digital divide of physical access over time

These two patterns also occur at the level of *countries*. Figure 4.3 shows that countries in the first stages of physical access exhibit widening gaps between people with high or low income, education and age combined. These gaps begin to close after a second tipping point, when about 50 per cent of the population gain access. In the figure, the lower line represents older people with low education and low income and the upper line younger people with higher education and a high income. The average physical access of individual countries can be mapped at a particular time and place. For example, in 2018 developing countries such as Eritrea, Chad and Burundi would be at the bottom left of the figure, while South Korea and Northern European countries would be at the top right.

A summary of statistics about computer and Internet access shows that, between 1984 and 2002, the gaps in income, education, employment, ethnicity and age were indeed widening in the developed countries (van Dijk 2005: 51–2). Between 2003 and 2006 these gaps started to close in these countries (see regular surveys by, among others, the Pew Research Center and NTIA in the US and the Oxford Internet Institute in the UK). However, in 2018 these gaps are still widening *inside* the developing countries (see annual reports by the ITU and the UN's *World Development Reports*).

Two major conclusions can be arrived at in the shape of expectations:

1   Near universal access to a *basic* computer and Internet connection should be available to the vast majority of the population in developed countries within one or two decades. However, if the stratification

pattern holds, 'near' universal access might mean that 10 per cent or more of the population still have no access. In the developing countries, on the other hand, near universal access might take two or three decades, and in the meantime a stratification pattern will account for perhaps a quarter or third of the population being excluded.

2   However, the digital divide of physical access is here to stay in another guise. Increasingly, having basic hardware and a slow connection is not enough for an individual to be included in the digital world. General material access and specific conditional access will become more important. This does not mean that hardware is no longer a problem. On the contrary, its quality or capacity, its diversity and continuous replacement and maintenance will create new physical access divides.

The final conclusion is that closing the gaps in physical access will not put an end to the digital divide: there will remain inequality in skills and usage, which I will now discuss.

5 Digital and Twenty-First-Century Skills

Introduction: who is able to deal with digital media?

Learning how to work with digital technology is a crucial step. Researchers in the early twenty-first century understood that skills and usage would become their primary focus, and Eszter Hargittai (2002) framed this research as the second-level digital divide.

This does not mean that, in the 1980s and 1990s, the operation and management of computers and Internet connections was believed to be unimportant. On the contrary, computers were not considered to be user-friendly machines. Indeed, in the 1960s and 1970s only experts and programmers were able to handle them. Even when the general population started to work with PCs in the 1990s, their operation was still thought to be more difficult than that of other media.

In the first decade of the twenty-first century the capacity to work effectively with digital media was extended with *content*-related skills, as people began working with sources of information and communication. Twenty-first-century skills are problem-solving and decision-making, critical thinking, creativity, and cooperating with peers or in teamwork.

The following section will deal with the various concepts of these skills. I will explain why I prefer the term skills rather than competencies, capabilities, literacies or other terms. The early twenty-first century was marked by numerous attempts to find a *framework* for digital skills, competencies or literacies. I shall explain some of these frameworks and discuss the similarities and differences between digital skills and traditional media skills or literacies. Finally, I will ask whether digital skills are learned in formal courses and training or whether they are developed via informal social and public support and through self-study or practice.

The third section summarizes research into why people have different levels of digital skills. The causes are comparable with those we found in the stages of motivation or attitude and physical access. Are the same resources, positional and personal categories effective in the gaps in digital skills?

I will then explore the consequences of the differences of levels of digital skills. How do they affect the uses and outcomes of digital media? Will people with low levels of skill be excluded from society? Will a highly skilled information elite secure the best jobs and decide what happens in society?

The final section draws together the potential trends in the evolution of digital skills. Will ever more demanding and advanced skills be required in the future for employees, citizens and consumers, or will they be simplified because apparently accessible devices such as tablets are offered and because a growing number of applications work autonomously? Will the most recent skills be required for all people in the information and network society or for an information elite only?

Basic concepts

The core term

There are many terms that designate the individual ability to operate and use digital media. In the last twenty-five years those found most often are literacy, competence, capability, fluency, skill, and computer or web knowledge. The first term proposed in the 1980s and 1990s was *computer literacy*. Tobin (1983: 22) defined this simply as 'the ability to utilize the capabilities of computers intelligently'. At the end of the 1990s Gilster (1997) extended this term to become *digital literacy*, which he defined as the usage and comprehension of information in the age of digital technologies – which means more than just computers.

Literacy is probably the most frequently used term, in combination with various adjectives: computer literacy, media literacy, digital literacy, information literacy and many others. The word 'literacy' has the connotations of reading or writing texts and cognitive processes such as understanding. However, researchers using this as the core term are also employing it for more comprehensive meanings (Bawden 2008). Media literacy, for example, is much broader than computer and digital literacy (Potter [1998] 2008; Hobbs 2011); it means being able to access, analyse, evaluate and create messages in a wide variety of media, including traditional media. It is often a normative concept too, because audiences are supposed to be critical in using media and their messages, and children in school have to be educated accordingly.

Competency is the most general term on the list. It often means having the capacity to evaluate knowledge appropriately and apply it pragmatically (Anttiroiko et al. 2001), notably in computer-mediated communication (Bubaš and Hutinski 2003; Spitzberg 2006) and in general Internet use (Carretero et al. 2017).

The most specific term is *digital skills or e-skills*, which focuses on (inter) action rather than on knowledge and its application. This interaction is with programs and web sources, as well as with other people (communication); it enables the transaction of goods and services and involves making decisions continually (van Dijk and van Deursen 2014: 140). Because the concepts of knowledge and literacy are so strongly associated with using more traditional media, I prefer to use the core term 'digital skills' in this book. However, in specifying these skills, I will show that particular knowledge and literacy are also necessary in order to attain specific goals in digital media use.

Literacy, competence or skill for which digital media?

In the previous chapter it was observed that there is an increasing diversity in types of digital media. To which of these do the concepts of digital literacies, competencies and skills apply? Working with advanced PCs, laptops, smartphones, feature phones, wearables, game consoles, Internet television and the Internet in general require different abilities. Some researchers refer to computer literacy, others to Internet skills. Most focus on one type of device and connection. In this chapter I propose a general framework of digital skills that applies to all digital media but concentrates on Internet skills, because it is the Internet that links and integrates all devices and connections.

The importance of technology change

Researchers into digital literacy, competence and skill are confronted with continual technological change. The evolution from PC to laptop to tablet, although retaining the same information and communication tasks, has demanded new skills of the user. The advent of the Internet of Things, marked by autonomous devices and systems, also requires fresh expertise: people have to evaluate and control these automatic decisions. Such examples demonstrate that digital literacy research has to react to a moving target of technological change.

General frameworks of digital literacy, competence and skill

In the last fifteen years multiple general frameworks, covering all digital literacies, competencies and skills, have been constructed and proposed to the scholarly and policy community (see summaries in van Deursen 2010; Litt 2013; and van Dijk and van Deursen 2014). It is very important to define any target group of people requiring these literacies or skills. In formal education they will be students, whose learning goals can be specified. In adult education, for instance, it might be the modules of a computer driving licence offered by training institutions in many countries. Training courses for employees can be designed for particular work tasks. For the general population, tuition in online digital skills is sometimes offered by local authorities and other organizations. Unfortunately, it is likely that businesses believe that their relatively simple and standard websites are easily managed by all consumers.

In this chapter I am concerned with basic digital media skills or competencies for the general public and, so, to establish a comprehensive framework *aimed at everyone* who wants to use a computer or phone with an Internet connection.

There are numerous proposals of such frameworks which cannot be discussed fully in this section. From 2001, Bawden formulated a number of very general 'new literacies', consisting of computer literacy, general information literacy, digital information literacy, network literacy and media literacy (Bawden and Robinson 2001; Bawden 2008). Warschauer (2003) offered five specific literacies: computer literacy (basic forms of computer and network operation), information literacy (the ability to manage vast amounts of information), multi-media literacy (the ability to understand and produce multi-media content) and computer-mediated literacy (managing applications such as e-mail, chatting and video-conferencing, and practising 'netiquette'). Amichai-Hamburger et al. (2004) published the first experiments with assessments of five literacies: photo-visual (reading computer and Internet graphics), reproduction (to create new content from older material), information (evaluating information), branching (reading non-linear hyper-texts) and socio-emotional literacy (understanding the rules of Internet discourse), while Livingstone et al. (2005) offered a very broad list of literacy items for adults specified for every medium, both traditional and digital. Later, Livingstone and Helsper (2007, 2010) concentrated on Internet literacies and skills for children and teenagers.

A framework based on *competencies* was first proposed by Gilster (1997), who listed ten very general competencies, ranging from problem-solving and searching skills to critical judgement of contents found online and understanding network tools and hyper-text. Spitzberg (2006) itemized competencies of communication in e-mail and on the Internet. Finally, I come to *The Digital Competence Framework for Citizens*, by Carretero, Vuorikari and Punie (2017), published by the European Commission.

The authors propose five general competence areas: information and data literacy, communication and cooperation, digital content creation, safety, and problem-solving.

The tradition of using *skills* as the core theme in research started with Hargittai (2002), who interviewed and assessed fifty-four randomly sampled Internet users in observational sessions and gave them tasks to find several types of information online. Bunz (2004) also asked for operational skills in using e-mail and websites to create a so-called computer–e-mail–web fluency scale. Van Dijk (2003, 2005) also proposed a framework to observe digital skills, which was elaborated and extended by van Deursen (2010) and fully described in the book *Digital Skills: Unlocking the Information Society* (van Dijk and van Deursen 2014). A summary is provided below.

Research strategies to investigate digital literacy, competence or skill

The basic concepts of digital literacy, competence and skill acquire different meanings through the ways in which they are observed, whether surveys, interviews, assessments or tests, and ethnography or field research.

The most frequent strategy is to conduct a survey with printed or online questionnaires or with interviews. Respondents are asked to report on their computer and Internet behaviour and rate their own performance in terms of literacy, competence and skills. Unfortunately, this strategy is poor in validity: most people overrate their performance, and males, especially young males, rate themselves higher than do females.

A relatively better type of survey is to ask proxy questions about the tasks, steps or procedures people have actually accomplished through using computers and the Internet. But the best strategy in validity and reliability is direct observation of performance. Hargittai (2002) Alkali and Amichai-Hamburger (2004) and van Deursen (2010) charged subjects in laboratory settings with tasks such as finding something on the Internet. The problems with this strategy are that it is very laborious and expensive and that only a small sample of subjects can be measured. So, in practice, researchers often turn to proxy questions in surveys.

The third strategy is ethnography or field observation. This means observing Internet users both online and offline and then interviewing them (Leander 2007). Tripp (2011) observed the Internet skills of Latino parents and children both at home and in the classroom, interviewed them, and analysed children's homework for potential skills developed. This strategy offers a wide perspective of literacies or skills in the social context, but it involves only micro-settings and so presents no chance of generalization.

The specific framework of digital skills used in this book

In this section, my own general framework, developed in the last fifteen years with my colleague Alexander van Deursen, will be used for the following reasons to describe the most important specific digital skills (van Dijk 2005; van Deursen 2010; van Dijk and van Deursen 2014). First, all specific digital skills discussed in the remainder of the book can be directly related to this framework. Second, the framework is broad enough to cover most of the other literacies, competencies and skills previously mentioned. Third, it has been validated in several empirical laboratory assessments with representative groups of the Dutch population, in skill tests for employees, and in surveys with proxy questions for specific skills. Currently, it is being used in several international research projects, as it is part of the larger 'from digital skills to tangible outcomes' (DiSTO) approach (see www.lse.ac.uk/media-and-communications/research/research-projects/disto).

Before describing our framework, I have to explain that it follows a particular approach. The notion of digital skills is instrumental. While literacies focus on the perception, understanding and creation of contents and competencies on potential use and its results, skills concentrate on what users can *actually do* with and within digital media. They act and react with hardware, software and applications for a particular goal. The question is whether or not they are successful.

The framework has four other general characteristics (van Dijk and van Deursen 2014: 141):

- A distinction is made between medium- and content-related skills.
- This distinction is sequential and conditional: without sufficient medium-related skills, content-related skills cannot be accomplished.
- The framework is empirical and not normative. For example, to assess information skills, only the accuracy and validity of information found in online sources and via search engines are evaluated.
- So far, the framework has been applied mainly to Internet skills, although it can easily be adapted to other (digital) media.

Special medium-related skills are involved in the use of digital media. For computers, the first requirement is *operational skills*. Users need to command keyboards and all kinds of peripherals, and they have to learn the interfaces of all programs and content, particularly operating systems and applications. Additionally, they need to understand the formal structures of the medium. Just like books, with their chapters, paragraphs, notes and indexes, computers and the Internet have specific structures. Computers have maps, files, menus and access codes and the Internet has websites, hyperlinks, fields for addresses and searches, and many other special entries. Browsing and navigating on the Internet is not as straightforward as people tend to believe. Obtaining the *formal skills* to find your way around the Internet requires exploration and practice.

In the 1990s these operational and formal skills were mainly understood as abilities of a technical kind, command of which was believed to solve the skill problem. In the first decade of the twenty-first century, information literacy, competence or skill was added to the mix. *Information skill* – the ability to search, select and evaluate information online – is the first and most important of these and involves, for instance, a systematic and accurate use of search engines. The evaluation of information is a critical accomplishment. An example is tackling disinformation or 'fake news'. An empirical approach towards evaluating information might detect only specific statements as being evidently 'fake'; a normative approach encounters problems in evaluating many more statements because almost every news item is biased to a certain extent.

Communication skills involve the effective use of e-mail and other message applications and the ability to contact people online successfully, to construct an attractive profile online, and exchange information or give opinions. Such skills are becoming more and more important in the network society.

The third type of content-related skill is *content-creating skill*. Most people contributing to the web are amateur writers, moviemakers and musicians, not professionals, and the quality of what they produce is highly diverse. A minimum of writing and creation skills is required to be effective and attractive in a web environment.

The last type of digital skill, and the one most difficult to achieve, is the *strategic skill* of using the Internet as a means to reach a particular professional and personal goal. Strategic skills require the mastering of all the other skills. None of the four content-related skills can be deployed without sufficient operational and formal skills, and strategic skills cannot be achieved without information, communication and content-related skills. Additional strategic operations are needed to work with privacy settings and security aids on the Internet.

I will give two examples of professional and personal goals. Writing a letter or application for a job requires first the information skill to find that suitable post among the many thousand online. Communication skill

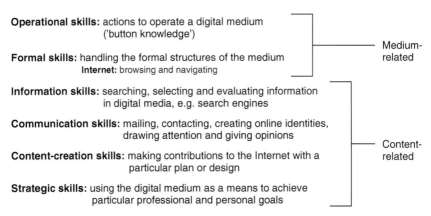

Figure 5.1. A general framework of six medium- and content-related digital skills

is needed to write an e-mail introducing a convincing application letter, and content-creating skill is necessary to write the letter and to generate an effective job profile. Second1ly, looking for a partner though online dating needs information skill to select the preferred candidate from a huge pool of contenders, content-creating skill to represent an attractive profile, and communication skill to write an effective introduction or invitation in order to realize the strategic skill of addressing the best match available.

These six conditional and sequential skills are summarized in figure 5.1. Medium-related skills are needed to realize content-related skills. In a wealthy country such as the Netherlands, with 98 per cent Internet access, the majority of the population has sufficient medium-related skills, but most strategic skills are mastered by only about 20 per cent of the population (van Deursen 2010, van Deursen and van Dijk 2015a). The six digital skills of the framework are specified for the Internet by van Dijk and van Deursen (2014: 42).

Causes of divides in digital skills

Divides in digital skills can be explained by people's resources and positional or personal categories. Digital skills primarily require cognitive characteristics such as intelligence, knowledge and technical ability, though motivation also remains important.

Resources supporting digital skills

Evidently, if people do not have sufficient *material and temporal resources*, they will not develop digital skills. However, we will see that, while considerable Internet experience is likely to support medium-related skills, there is no guarantee that it will help develop content-related skills (van Deursen and van Dijk 2011).

Mental, social and cultural resources, then, are more important for explaining differences in people's digital skills. Mental resources – technical proficiency or know-how, knowledge of technological and societal affairs, and analytic capabilities – are the most significant. Søby (2003), Mossberger et al. (2003) and Carvin (2000) found that technical proficiency or competence – an accumulated knowledge of hardware, software, applications and connections – is a basic component of digital literacy. It is well known that people turn to tech-savvies to help them with technical problems.

Most people do not develop digital skills on their own, and their social context is very relevant when they meet problems and require assistance. However, not everyone benefits from the *social resources* of colleagues, family members and friends with better skills or is able to consult a help desk or find a computer course.

Figure 5.2 shows the various ways of acquiring computer and Internet skills in the European Union. Unfortunately, the statistics date from 2011, but in my estimation they are an indication of a distribution that still holds,

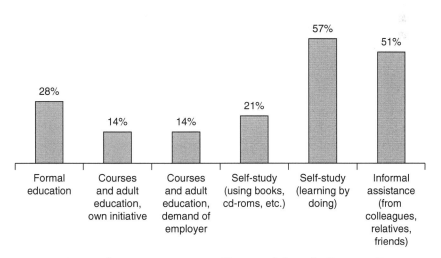

Figure 5.2. Ways of acquiring computer and Internet skills in the European Union
Source: Eurostat, *Internet Use in Households and by Individuals in 2011*.

and not only in the EU but also elsewhere. The figure shows that informal ways of acquiring digital skills are much more important than formal ways, Seeking social support from others is the second most common course of action.

Van Deursen et al. (2014) created a typology of users acquiring digital skills and, in a representative survey of the Dutch population, found that their characteristics confirmed the distribution shown in figure 5.2. The first group, *the independents*, learn skills by doing or through trial and error, though they might also make use of manuals, DVDs or websites. This type significantly consists largely of young, male and highly educated people. The second group, the *socially supported*, ask colleagues, relatives and friends for assistance when they find a problem. This type is made up mainly of seniors, females and people with low education. The third group are the *formal help seekers*, who follow classes of formal adult education or special computer classes and courses, either on their own initiative or via their employer. They also consult computer experts and help desks. Formal help seekers are mainly employed, relatively old, and have followed low- or medium-level education.

According to surveys, the independents have the highest levels of all kinds of skills. The socially supported learn some operational and formal skills but no information or strategic skills. This mode of learning is unreliable because relatives or friends often provide partial or wrong solutions and answers. Thus, the socially supported are the worst performers, even in operational and formal skills. Unfortunately, people with the lowest digital skills obtain the worst social support (Helsper and van Deursen 2017; van Deursen et al. 2014). Formal help seekers obtain information and strategic skills in their courses and classes.

As far as *cultural resources* are concerned, a *lifestyle* that involves using digital media throughout the day, and for every imaginable purpose, makes it easier for such 'digirati' to develop their skills (Ragnedda 2017), especially operational and formal skills. The *status* earned by an expert in the operation of ICT stimulates their motivation to maintain their reputation by acquiring even more skills. Advising people also helps such experts to have a better understanding of problems. Finally, *status markers* motivate owners who have purchased a number of flashy new devices and apps to master them thoroughly in order to demonstrate them to others.

Positional categories determining resources and digital skills

The first series of background factors determining all these resources are positional categories. In all observations of digital skills, literacies or competencies, by both assessments and proxy survey questions, the *attainment of education*, whether in school or via adult education, is the most important factor (Bonfadelli 2002; Gui and Argentin 2011; Hargittai 2010; van Deursen 2010; van Deursen and van Dijk 2009, 2011, 2015b). Van Deursen (2010) and van Deursen and van Dijk (2009, 2011) have found in both laboratory assessments and surveys that people with higher education perform better, particularly in content-related skills and strategic decision-making.

An individual's *labour position* is the second important category explaining differences in digital skills. Clearly, people with a job that requires the use of computers have more opportunities to improve their skills (van Deursen and van Dijk 2012).

On average people in a developing country have fewer opportunities to learn digital skills, even when they are part of the elite, than people in a developed country. The availability and quality of a *nation or region*'s information and communication infrastructure, together with its educational institutions, dictate the opportunities available to the population. Unfortunately, there is no international comparative research concerning the level of digital skills attained by different countries. Institutions such as the World Bank (2016), the Economist Intelligence Unit (2019) and Unesco (Broadband Commission et al. 2017) have tried to estimate the national level of digital skills mainly through educational performance.

People living in multi-person *households* clearly have more opportunities to improve their skills. In particular, parents can help their children with content-related skills, though many children have better medium-related skills than their parents.

The final category is a position in *a social network*. People with large social networks are the first to receive strategic information from others in their circle (Kadushin 2012), a position that allows them to 'hoard' all kinds of opportunities (Tilly 1998). In every society there is a big overlap between the information elite and the social, economic, political and cultural elite.

Personal categories determining resources and digital skills

The most important personal category determining technical proficiency, knowledge and analytic capabilities is *intelligence and the technical ability* to understand and operate digital technology. Unfortunately, these have not been directly measured in digital divide research, where IQ tests are rarely conducted. Intelligence and technical ability are sometimes tested in research in computer classes and the like in schools. However, the results are

71

valid only for the particular course and not for the levels of intelligence and digital skills in the general population.

In my view, digital divide research has turned a blind eye to the importance of intelligence. In most research, education has been found to be the most significant background factor in the digital divide and so is the most important key to solving this problem. However, what actually explains the role of education in differences in skill?

Whether we like it or not, natural science has shown that intelligence is partly hereditary (Lee et al. 2018). *Intelligence* is related to the ability to process information. According to Guilford (1967), this requires five mental operations: 1) to recognize information quickly and to give it meaning, 2) to recall information immediately, 3) to find many solutions to problems, 4) to bring different things in a common denominator and 5) to evaluate information to make a judgement. Clearly, these mental operations are needed for content-related digital skills, especially information and strategic skills.

Technical ability is a kind of practical intelligence related more to medium-related than to content-related skills. At all levels of education some people are more tech-savvy – 'being good at computers' and the like – than others.

In contrast to the other personal categories, *age* is frequently investigated in digital skills research. The general conclusion is that young people are better than older people in medium-related digital skills, but the results are mixed as far as content-related skills are concerned (Litt 2013). A popular notion is that young people are better at using digital media and the Internet, and new terms have been created to describe them, such as 'digital natives' and 'net generation' (Tapscott 1998; Prensky 2001). However, this notion largely is a myth: in fact, the level of digital skills among the young generation is very wide-ranging (Hargittai and Hinnant 2008; Hargittai 2010; Helsper and Eynon 2010; Calvani et al. 2012). What is more surprising is that research has shown that older generations might be better at using the Internet than the young! This is explained by the fact that young people have better medium-related skills such as 'button knowledge' and fast navigation, while seniors have superior content-related skills (provided that they have sufficient medium-related skills to start with). Figure 5.3 is a causal model of the results of a representative Dutch survey that supports these statements (though note that communication and content-creating skills were not measured in this survey). The figure shows that increasing age has a negative impact on medium-related skills and a positive effect on content-related skills. While older people have less Internet experience and spend fewer hours online than young

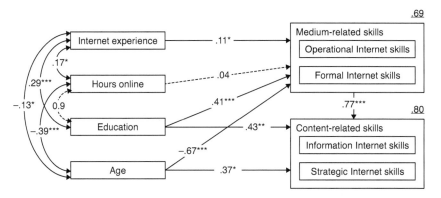

Figure 5.3. Causal path model of four independent factors explaining digital skills
Source: van Deursen et al. (2011).

people, experience is barely significant and the number of hours spent online is not meaningful. Adequate medium-related skills are needed for content-related digital skills to be developed. Finally, the figure shows that age and education are very important personal categories affecting the level of digital skills. These results have been confirmed in other countries by Alkali and Amichchai-Hamburger (2004), Helsper and Eynon (2010) and Gui and Argentin (2011).

Gender is the third personal category often investigated in digital skills research, though most does not find significant differences between the skills of males and females (Litt 2013) – at least, not in advanced high-tech countries. The situation might well be different in developing nations and in countries where there is a lack of female emancipation. I have already stated in this book that people, especially (young) males, overrate the level of their skills as compared to the objective results of tests. Just before conducting his laboratory assessments, van Deursen (2010) gave a questionnaire to all participants and asked them to rate their own level of skill. While males rated their expertise at a much higher level than did females, the actual performance of both in the assessment was shown to be equal. The same observation was also made by Hargittai and Shafer (2006) and Hargittai and Hinnant (2008).

The last personal categories to be discussed are *health or disability and illiteracy*. Disabled people are less likely to go online than the able-bodied (Dobransky and Hargittai 2016), and the disabled on average show lower levels of skill (van der Geest et al. 2014; van Dijk and Van Deursen 2014: 129–31). Complete and functional illiterates will have no content-related and very few medium-related digital skills since they cannot handle words, documents or the names of menus or links. The *Human Development Report*

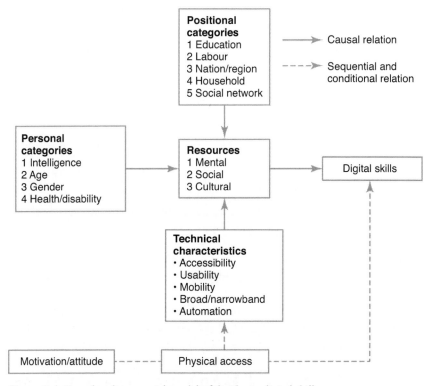

Figure 5.4. Causal and sequential model of divides in digital skills

2009 (UNDP 2009) estimated the proportion of functional illiterates to be 20 per cent in the US, 22 per cent in the UK and 7.5 per cent in Sweden (the lowest figure). The number of illiterate people in modern society, let alone in the information and network society, is a persisting problem that is very difficult to solve.

The various causes of inequality in digital skills are shown in figure 5.4. The order of factors in the boxes is estimated.

Technical characteristics

Finally, there are a number of technical characteristics of contemporary digital media that affect the possibility of developing digital skills. The first of these is *accessibility*. Being able to access the same kind of hardware, software and applications – for instance at work, in school, at home, while commuting or at public access points – is particularly helpful when one is learning digital skills. Taking advantage of mobile access at all times is an option. However, many applications can better be performed on PCs or laptops, with their bigger screens, keyboards and often faster connections (see the characteristic of mobility below).

The second characteristic is *usability* – the ease of use and learnability of the hardware, software and applications. Shneiderman (1980) and Nielsen (1994) have created a framework for usability with the following attributes: learnability (the ease of accomplishing a basic task), efficiency (how quickly this task may be performed), memorability (remembering how to carry out a certain task), correction of errors (how many errors are made and how they can be recovered) and satisfaction (the pleasure of using the tool). All of these affect the learning of digital skills.

Another characteristic of usability is the intuitiveness of a device or application. Tablets and smartphones are relatively easy to use instinctively by, for example, dragging horizontally or vertically across the screen with your finger. Intuitive use can help with the development of medium-related skills. However, ease of use also is deceptive: it both seduces us to avoid learning more difficult content-related skills (van Dijk and van Deursen 2014: 99–101; van Deursen et al. 2016), and it stimulates constant following, swiping and tapping on links, words or pictures presented on the screen rather than encouraging input of content by users themselves.

The third technical characteristic is *mobility*. This offers the same trade-offs as usability. People who are able use the same digital media at all times and in all places have more chances of learning the required medium-related skills. However, users tend to avoid the more advanced applications offered on PCs and laptops (Bao et al. 2011; Napoli and Obar 2014), meaning that they also learn fewer content-related skills (van Deursen and van Dijk 2019). (See more about this in chapter 6.) Broadband as compared to narrowband connections do not show the same trade-off. Broadband is always better for both medium- and content-related skills, as many more visual cues of understanding are presented and many more and diverse advanced applications are offered (Mossberger et al. 2012). Pictures and videos can be downloaded and uploaded quickly and response times in all interfaces are much shorter.

The final important technical characteristic is *automation*. More and more applications are now offered that work on the basis of artificial intelligence. In the context of the Internet of Things, augmented reality and personal assistants (provided in search engines or with smart home devices), more and more decisions are made via algorithms. Users need to learn only a few additional operational skills to utilize their health and sport wearables, smart watches and glasses, self-driving cars, energy meters at home, online heating and kitchen remote controls, search engines for assistance, and many others. The devices and their intelligent software do all the work.

This means that information, communication and content-creation skills would seem to be less important. Even strategic skills may no longer be needed when smart applications take the decisions. However, in truth they are needed more (van Deursen and Mossberger 2018). Users need to know first whether it is actually smart to purchase these applications and whether the decisions made would be their own preferred decisions. Using these technologies people are additionally confronted with *systems* – transport systems, energy provision, health care and assurance systems, and provider systems of platforms such as Google. Understanding these systems requires more knowledge than most people actually possess. In fact, advanced strategic skills are needed, a type of content-related skill least performed by the average user (see above). Again, this technical characteristic is a trade-off of a technology that makes it both easier and more difficult for users to learn the required digital skills.

The consequences of divides in digital skills

Having sufficient digital skills is a turning point in the whole process of adopting technology. It is most likely that people with a high level of digital skills will be the most frequent users of all types of media, while those with a low level of skills will use them only for relatively simple or attractive tasks such as personal communication, e-shopping and entertainment. The final result is that such people will gain fewer benefits and those with a high level of digital skills will benefit more and suffer less harm from its negative aspects (security and privacy problems, cybercrime, cyberbullying and other abuse; see chapter 7).

The causal links between digital skills, frequency and diversity of use, and positive or negative outcomes are demonstrated in nationwide survey results from several countries (Helsper 2012; Pearce and Rice 2013; van Deursen and van Dijk 2015b; van Deursen and Helsper 2015; van Deursen et al. 2017).

Another consequence of the differences in mastering digital skills is that the already strong position of the *information elite* in society, the professional-managerial class, academics, government officials and businessmen, will become reinforced (Michaels et al. 2014). Conversely, the already feeble position of people with low education in manual or unskilled jobs will become even weaker in an information society. Such workers are at permanent risk of their jobs being eliminated by automation and robotization; their wages tend to stagnate or be cut. In the meantime, people with higher education and average or advanced ICT skills earn a 'skills premium' (Nahuis and de Groot 2003); these skills are substantially rewarded in the labour market (Falck et al. 2016; O'Mahoney et al. 2008). The use of ICT has polarized skills demand in the last twenty-five years: instead of requiring staff with medium-level education, industries now call for people with higher education and high digital skills (Michaels et al. 2014).

A similar polarization occurs among those enrolling in educational institutions. The higher the level of courses, the greater are the digital skills needed to follow the programme of study and to succeed in exams. Today, it is impossible to pursue higher education without sufficient digital skills.

The evolution in the level and nature of digital skills

In the last ten years the *absolute* levels of digital skills attained by the general public have increased, as have the *relative* differences in skills attained by particular groups (van Deursen and van Dijk 2015a). This means that people of every social class, age and gender, and with all levels of education, have developed higher skills, especially medium-related skills. However, relative gaps in mastering digital skills between those at the higher and lower ends of educational attainment and labour position have also grown, though they do not seem to occur as far as gender and age are concerned: females and seniors are now catching up with males and the young, at least in the developing counties.

Two opposing trends will decide the future of digital skills. The first consists of the growing *requirements* that our societies and advanced technologies impose on the use of ICT: the complexity of both is increasing. More and more difficult tasks are set for and performed by digital media in all ways of life. These tasks require much information processing, abstract thinking and strategic decision-making, meaning that the necessity for content-related skills will increase.

The other trend is composed of the *affordances* of new technology: new methods of carrying out existing tasks will tend to require simpler skills. Speech and face recognition, replacing the need to use keyboards, and images and speaking inputs and outputs replacing texts will reduce the demands on medium-related skills. For example, instead of using a textual search engine, individuals can speak to a 'personal assistant'. New artificial intelligence software will help users to make decisions, thus reducing the requirements of content-related skills. However, the operations and communications performed by digital technology will not be reduced: people, organizations and societies want more and more complex tasks to be carried out in this manner. For example, the advent of the Internet of Things might lead to fewer demands on medium-related skills but more demands on making decisions about the acceptance of the advice given and the service of the systems offering such applications (van Deursen and Mossberger 2018). Will I accept the advice of my wearable smart watch to take more steps a day? Is it wise to transmit the data provided by this device concerning my performance to my doctor and health insurer? More strategic digital skills are needed for this purpose than before.

The demands on content-related digital skills are also increasing on account of the requirements of so-called *twenty-first-century skills*. These substantial cognitive and behavioural skills are very similar to content-related digital skills. The most popular frameworks have been made by the Partnership for 21st Century Skills (2008) and Binkley et al. (2012). Following a systematic literature review, van Laar et al. (2017) created a list of core twenty-first-century *digital* skills (see figure 5.5). These authors also found some additional skills in the literature – self-direction, ethical and cultural awareness, lifelong learning skills and flexibility skills – though these will not be discussed here.

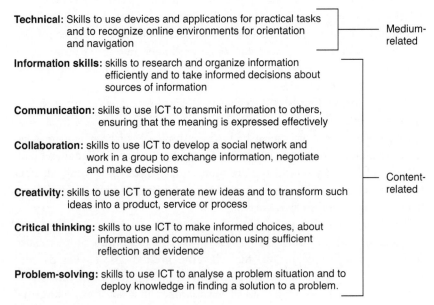

Figure 5.5. Framework of core twenty-first-century skills
Source: Adapted from van Laar et al. (2017: 583).

These seven core skills are content-related, and digital media or ICTs are among the most important tools to realize these skills. Today there are effective, reliable and valid search engines, online personal assistants and other applications to find, process and evaluate online information. Communication these days requires an appropriate and effective use of e-mail, social-networking sites and messaging services. Collaboration often involves content management systems, wikis, document cooperation among groups, and chat platforms. Creativity can be enhanced by an appropriate use of tools to devise online content. Critical thinking, defined as observable informed choices, is required in using search tools and evaluating any information or disinformation on the web. Problem-solving skills can be improved by an effective use of various online tools, from search consoles (advanced search engines) to development apps.

It is to be expected that professional workers, e-participating citizens and experienced e-commerce consumers with a high level of educational attainment will be the first to develop these twenty-first-century skills, but this is not yet supported by empirical research. Meanwhile the need for medium-related skills at a basic level will continue or even be reduced. We should bear in mind, however, that the number of digital devices and programs is multiplying with the rise of the Internet of Things and virtual or augmented reality, all of which require a number of additional operational skills.

6   Usage Inequality

Introduction: who frequently and variously uses digital media?

Now we have reached the last phase in the process of full adoption of digital media. The goal is to use these media for a particular purpose of information, communication, transaction or entertainment. Accomplishing the three former phases is a necessary condition for usage: without sufficient motivation and at least a minimal positive attitude, without achieving physical access, and without developing sufficient digital skills, any digital media use will be absent or marginal.

However, these conditions are not sufficient for actual usage. For example, people may have access to digital media in their household or on other places but never use them. They might be forced to use them without any imagination. They might have particular digital skills but not exploit them because they prefer traditional media or find no occasion to use digital media. Unfortunately, in statistics about Internet and computer usage, physical access – for instance in households – often is conflated with use. Usage has its own grounds that will be discussed in this chapter.

Usage of digital media is affected by the occasion, the obligation, the available time and the necessary effort expended. It depends on *the tasks* people have and *the contexts* in which they are living. In the last two decades the tasks have multiplied and the contexts now embrace all spheres of daily life. Because the nature of the contexts is different – social, economic, cultural and technological – the aspects of digital media usage to be discussed in this chapter are different too.

The chapter will start with the basic concepts of usage, for which several typologies have been created. The most important are the *frequency and amount of use, use diversity* and *the activity of use* (creation or consumption).

The second section will list *the causes* of frequency, diversity and the activity of use of digital media, including the new devices of the Internet of Things and augmented or virtual reality. The core section of this chapter, as in the previous chapters, follows the general model of resources and appropriation theory (resources, positional or personal categories, and the technical properties of the media).

I shall then examine the *consequences* for (in)equality of all the divides of usage observed in the previous section. Will they disappear when the diffusion of digital media in society is absolute and universal access has been achieved? Or will they persist and become a permanent characteristic of future societies?

The final section will discuss the evolution of the usage divides. This is not only about their disappearance or persistence but also about their nature. Will they be generational (age), cultural (gender, ethnicity and lifestyle), social (social class and status), educational (knowledge, intelligence and competency) or economic (employment or own business and career)?

Basic concepts

Use typologies

How can the extreme variation in Internet use be conceptualized and classified? There are two popular approaches: one is to derive a typology from the core concepts of a theory and the other is a description induced by factor or cluster analysis. Both approaches produce suitable typologies and classifications. The usual theoretical approach is one of the technology acceptance theories (see chapter 2). The uses and gratification theory (Katz et al. 1973; Flanagin and Metzger 2001) lists a number of needs, motivations and gratifications that lead to a typology of Internet or other digital media use (see table 3.2, p. 37, where the items in the column of specific gratifications look like a number of digital media or Internet applications). The technology acceptance theory (Davis 1989), however, has not yet produced a use typology. Finally, the social cognitive theory, among others creating a media attendance model (LaRose and Eastin 2004), offers a number of expected outcomes, such as monetary, novelty, social and status outcomes, which look like particular applications.

The resources and appropriation theory, used as a framework to present digital divide research in this book, has also not produced a user typology because this theory focuses on independent causes rather than dependent applications of use.

In order to find a neutral typology of digital media and Internet use, the second approach is better. Here the point of departure is observable

Table 6.1. Typology of Internet use domains, activities and applications

Use domains	Activities	Internet applications
Work, study/ information use	Work	Professional applications
	Consumption	E-shopping and marketplaces
	Finance	Internet banking
	Citizenship	E-government services
	Learning/study	Online courses and training
	Career development	Personal development/independent learning sources
	Searching for information	Search engines/personal assistants and encyclopaedias
	Searching for news	News services/blogs
Leisure/social use	Communicating	E-mail/messaging services
	Networking	Social-networking services
	Community-building	Community sites and forums
	Sharing	Music, video (sharing) sites
	Entertainment	Online broadcasting and video
	Gaming	Online gaming
	Exploring	Browsing

Source: Derived from Kalmus et al. (2011).

activities, not motivations, perceptions or expected outcomes. Livingstone and Helper (2007), Brandtzæg (2010), Blank and Groselj (2014) and van Deursen and van Dijk (2014a) were among the first to induce these typologies. However, Kalmus et al. (2011: 392) derived the most suitable typology from a factor analysis in a representative survey among the population of Estonia – a country known for its high Internet access and use. This typology inspired the list of activities shown in table 6.1. It can be extended with activities found in other surveys.

The most important distinction in the Kalmus typology and in table 6.1 is the dichotomy of the two main kinds of Internet domains: *work/study or information* and *leisure or social* use or activity. This distinction will become fairly important in the remainder of this chapter because unequal use of these domains will be shown to create structural divides.

Use indicators

How can we measure digital media use? There are three indicators often used in research (see also Blank and Groselj 2014):

- *Frequency of use and amount of time*: from a baseline of 'non-use', through 'low use', 'regular use' and 'broad use', the incidence and the number of hours during which people use the Internet, etc. (Reisdorf and Groselj 2017);
- *Diversity of use*: the number of different activities for which the Internet, etc., is used, for example as listed in table 6.1;
- *Activity of use*: creative (active) or consumptive (relatively passive).

The first two indicators will figure in the following sections about the causes and consequences of divides in digital media use. Unfortunately, the third will have to be largely ignored, as I have not found much data for this indicator.

Causes of divides in digital media use

Resources affecting digital media use

In discussing the inequalities observed in using digital media, I will follow the same concepts of the framework applied in the former chapters. The most significant causes are social and cultural resources, backed by sufficient material resources (income) and temporal resources (time), though mental resources are pertinent in the form of basic motivations (needs) and attitudes or beliefs in choosing particular applications of digital media. We will also see that personality and intelligence (cognitive and technical ability) affect digital media use.

The most important resources for digital media use are *social*; close to half of the Internet activities listed in table 6.1 can be called social. The social contexts in which people live may stimulate or reduce media activities (Selwyn 2003, Selwyn et al. 2006). People are often obliged in workplaces and schools to use particular digital media, and the network effect takes place in communities and families. Once there is a critical mass of users of a particular device, the rate of adoption creates further growth. This happened with e-mail, social-networking sites, messaging services and Internet access in general. The social context also determines the level of support people receive: those in dense social networks are more likely to use popular digital media than isolated or marginal members of society.

Cultural resources in the form of lifestyle affect digital media use. Some people work all day on a computer or smartphone, while others are involved in playing, gaming or gambling, continually watching YouTube videos and Netflix series, or perpetually chatting via messaging services. The use of digital media can also be inspired by the status acquired by sharing music and funny videos and pictures. While once the possession of a PC, an Internet connection or a mobile phone yielded status, today prestige is gained only by having the latest smartphone, a brand new app or game, a state of the art device for augmented or virtual reality, a very fast Internet connection, or a house fully equipped with advanced equipment.

Of course, *mental resources* in the form of positive motivations and attitudes continue to be relevant for frequency and type of digital media use. However, motivations and attitudes are not resources. The importance of such characteristics as personality, cognitive intelligence and technical ability, physical or mental disabilities, and literacy will be discussed below.

Material resources are needed to benefit from the incentives of the social context and the lifestyle, habits or hobbies and status aimed for. Companies or institutions need to invest sufficiently in the hardware, software and connections required for jobs where computers and the Internet would be advantageous. Similarly, if schools do not have adequate numbers of computers for students, and parents cannot afford to buy them for the home, the impetus will die. A 'digital' lifestyle and culture, together with status markers, might be attractive, but they are expensive to maintain.

Temporal resources are also required. Many hours are spent using computers and the Internet in workplaces and schools, depending on the type of job and study. Professionals may use them use them all day long, and individuals with flexible or temporary jobs need them more than those in permanent employment. Many people in the developed societies, particularly those unemployed or unable to work, spend much of their leisure time on the Internet.

Positional categories determining resources and digital media use

We now turn to the factors responsible for the inequality of the resources people have in using digital media. The overwhelming majority of surveys in digital divide research in the world show that the level of both education and employment, often correlated with the level of income, are the most important background factors for the frequency and variety of digital media use next to the positional categories of age and gender (see Ryan and Lewis 2017; Dutton and Reisdorf 2017; and Pew Research Center 2018 for the US; Blank and Groselj 2014; van Deursen and van Dijk 2014a; Reisdorf and Groselj 2017; Lindblom and Räsänen 2017; and Serrano-Cinca et al. 2018 for the UK and the EU; and Pew Research Center 2018 for the whole world). Research published by the Pew Center shows that levels of education make more of a difference in developing countries than in developed countries (Poushter et al. 2018: 12).

Those who gain a good education generally acquire a good job. Using digital media at school and then for homework extends both the frequency and the variety of use, including into leisure time, where more highly educated students use more information and career-related applications than those with less education (see below). *Education level* reinforces not only the social but also the cultural resources needed for digital media use. It increases the number and variety of social relationships for inspiration and support in the school environment and enhances a 'digital lifestyle' of heavy use, creating particular habits and status markers at home and elsewhere.

An individual's *labour position* determines how frequently they use digital media, as well as how diverse that usage is and whether it is active or passive. Most research shows that it is managers and professionals who make greater use of computers than people with executive, manual and physical jobs (see Lindblom and Räsänen 2017 for the UK, Finland and Greece). Among managers and professionals, digital media are increasingly the primary – perhaps even the only – tools of their work; for administrative workers, however, perhaps practising data entry all day, their frequency of use will be very high but the diversity and creative use will be low. In general, the employed and students use more digital media than the retired and the unemployed (see examples in Blank and Groselj (2014) for the UK and Serrano-Cinca et al. (2018) for Spain), except for the unemployed in the Netherlands, who use the Internet more often for leisure pursuits (van Deursen and van Dijk 2014a).

The third positional category affecting usage is in which *country* an individual lives in the world and whether they are in *an urban or rural region*. There is much inequality in the relevant infrastructure for access, as well as in the variety of digital media available, particularly between developed and developing countries. The distribution of Internet or smartphone users in the world was noted by researchers for the Pew Center in 2018 (see figure 6.1). The map shows that, of thirty-seven countries, North America, Europe and parts of the Asia-Pacific region have the most users and sub-Saharan Africa, India and Indonesia the fewest. The distribution corresponds closely with the general, economic (GDP), social inequality (Gini coefficient) and other levels of development often used as the positional categorization of these countries (World Bank 2016).

All nations reveal a significant internal divide in digital media use between urban and rural regions. Here the causes are the availability and quality of infrastructure, regional economic performance and poverty, levels of education and skills, and the preferences of local cultures (Salemink et al. 2017). In developing countries, even those who have a high level of education, occupation and income show lower use of digital media than people in developed countries in equivalent circumstances.

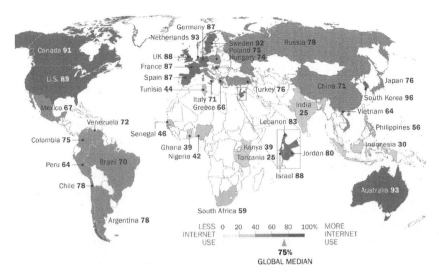

Figure 6.1. Percentages of adult Internet users or owners of a smartphone in thirty-seven countries of the world, 2017
Source: Poushter et al. (2018: 5).

A position in a *social network* will possibly affect digital media use too. However, I have found no empirical evidence of people having a central position in a large social network using digital media more than those with a small social network or in a marginal position. Both Tilly (2009) and Kadushin (2012) expect that the former find and hoard more opportunities – social media, messaging services and other online communication tools – than the latter. In earlier chapters I argued that social-network positions influence people's motivation, assistance in gaining physical access, and support in developing digital skills. Network analyses and surveys are required to show these differences.

Household position is less important, since both frequency and variety of digital media use are at about the same level in both single-person and multi-person households; only the type of applications might be different (see Blank and Grosjelj 2014 for the UK).

Personal categories determining resources and digital media use

Almost every research project concerning the digital divide shows that *age* is the most important personal cause of different use after the level of education attained. While 48 per cent of the total world population used the Internet in 2017, 70.6 per cent of that usage was by people aged fifteen to twenty-four. The percentage gap between overall usage and that of the younger population was the smallest in Europe (79.6 versus 95.7 per cent) and the biggest in Africa (21.8 versus 40.3 per cent). The poorer the country, the wider the gap; it is widest in the so-called least developed countries (LDCs) (ITU 2017).

Age can be categorized by *number of years*, by *generation* and by *life-stage*. The most popular and questionable category is that of generation, where a distinction is made between the Digital Natives and Immigrants. Digital Natives were born and grew up after the advent of the World Wide Web (1993), a generation also called the 'post-millennials', born from 1997 onwards. The distinction was coined by Prensky (2001) and Tapscott (1998), who suggested that members of this generation were not only much more frequent users of digital media than previous generations but also better in terms of their skills, the variety of their use and multitasking with other activities. This proposition was later supported by research undertaken, among others, by Zickuhr (2011) and Rosen (2012). However, it was also sincerely criticized in the research of Buckingham (2008), Hargittai and Hinnant (2008) and Helsper and Eynon (2010), who attempted to show that other factors, such as Internet experience, digital skills and types of use, were more important than generational effects. There are enormous differences in access, skills and usage among the so-called Digital Natives (Hargittai and Hinnant 2008), while older generations may well have better content-related digital skills than the young generation, who are certainly more adept at medium-related skills (van Deursen 2010; van Deursen and van Dijk 2014a; see chapter 5).

The distinction between generation and life-stage is decisive. Chesley and Johnson (2014) have analysed the differential use of digital media by generation and during the life course. They argue that we use digital media differently in childhood, adolescence, young adulthood, older adulthood and old age, and they also show that the generational effect is important. The age at which we are first introduced to digital media has consequences for the way in which we use it for the rest of our life.

This distinction is important because the generational effect in usage will slowly be reduced as time passes. At this point the older generations in the developed countries are catching up fast. However, life-stage effects are here to stay. Even fifty years from now adolescents will use digital media to help form their identity and communicate with their peers. Adults will use them primarily for organizing their lives, while elderly people will use them mostly for leisure, services such as health care, and communication with family and friends.

The second personal category affecting digital media use is *gender*. In the 1980s and 1990s it was (young) males who were the first to use digital media (van Dijk 2005). After the year 2000 the gender gaps in frequency of use became smaller, and by 2017 it had been reduced worldwide to 11.6 per cent (less for females). However, in Africa it was still 25.3 per cent and in the LDCs as a whole 32.9 per cent, though in the Americas women already used the Internet 2.6 per cent more than men (ITU 2017). The final figure shows that the gender gap is a direct result of the unfavourable conditions for women in several countries with respect to employment, education and income (Hilbert 2011; ITU 2017); in all countries where women participate in higher education, the gap in the frequency and variety of use disappears.

This does not mean that the differences in the types of use, such as particular Internet applications – see table 6.1, p. 82 – are declining (see Jackson et al. 2001; Schumacher and Morahan-Martin 2001; Zillien and Hargittai 2009; Blank and Groselj 2014; van Deursen and van Dijk 2014a; Martínez-Cantos 2017; and Sultana and Imtiaz 2018). The common denominator is that females are more likely to use communication and commercial applications and males information and entertainment applications (see the leisure or social use versus the work and information applications in table 6.1). However, in the future, when all social and cultural distinctions in society will be fully reflected in digital media use, these differences may be more clearly pronounced. See the arguments below and the following chapters.

The third important set of personal categories effecting digital media use consists of *intelligence, technical ability, literacy,* and *intellectual or physical disability.* Although we have insufficient empirical evidence to back up the assertion, people of low intelligence (superficially and perhaps arbitrarily measured as IQ), those who have little technical ability or expertise, the functionally illiterate and the disabled make less use of digital media and the Internet. Surveys dealing with digital media use have no questions as to IQ or other measures of intelligence or the ability of respondents, and performance tests do not examine intelligence by other measures. Correlations are established only with the level of education attained.

Nevertheless, I want to argue that intelligence, technical ability, literacy and disability are very important background measures of mental, social and cultural resources causing the divides of digital media use. The main reasons for such people finding digital media less attractive are the design, the interface and the content of websites, which are designed for intelligent and literate people who are able to operate a device and its applications and have no disabilities.

It is estimated that 2.2 per cent of the population in Western countries have an IQ below 70; 13.6 per cent are between 70 and 85, and two-thirds of the population are at the average quotient, between 85 and 115 (Urbina 2011; and Flanagan and Harrison 2012). Chadwick et al. (2013) discuss the barriers and the opportunities of the Internet for the learning disabled and those of low intelligence. Many such individuals who have Internet access in their home do not actually use it (see Gutiérrez and Martorell 2011 for Spain), largely on account of the design and content of websites (Wehmeyer 2004). The learning disabled are often 'infantilized' by their caregivers, who think that the Internet is bad or dangerous for them (Chadwick et al. 2013).

In the least-developed countries, more than 50 per cent of the population are illiterate (UNDP 2016), and as much as 20 per cent of the population in the US (32 million adults) and the UK (8 million) may be functionally illiterate, with comparable figures in other Western countries (see Ullah and Ullah 2014; UNDP 2016). Such people are only able to understand images or symbols and video or audio content.

Another large category is *the disabled*, who are estimated as being between 12 and 27 per cent of any population (Fox 2011; Anderson and Perrin). For example, in the US, 15 per cent of the adult population have problems in walking, 9 per cent in hearing and 7 per cent in seeing; 11 per cent have a serious condition affecting their ability to concentrate, remember or make decisions, and 9 per cent are unable to go shopping or visit the doctor without assistance. While in 2016 only 8 per cent of Americans had never used the Internet, 23 per cent of disabled Americans had never done so. In that year only 50 per cent of disabled Americans use the Internet on a daily basis while the overall population reported 79 per cent daily use (Anderson and Perrin 2017). According to a large-scale survey of 3,556 disabled individuals in Poland in 2013, only 33 per cent used the Internet, while the figure for the whole population was 63 per cent (Duplaga 2017). Even controlled for age, poverty and education, disability remains as a digital divide factor (Dobransky and Hargittai 2016; Anderson and Perrin 2017).

The last personal category to be mentioned is *personality*. Several studies suggest that, among the 'Big Five' personal characteristics, people with particular traits show more Internet engagement than others (Russo and Amnå 2016). The first, openness to experience (showing intellectual curiosity for a breadth of cultural phenomena, novel experiences and new ideas), inspires more Internet use than the more closed-minded, pragmatic, habitual or perseverant personality (Tuten and Bosnjak 2001; Vecchione and Caprara

2009; Gerber et al. 2011). Second, extroversion also inspires Internet use, especially for establishing contacts and partaking in discussions such as in social networking and using social media in general (Ryan and Xenos 2011). Third, the conscientious personality, who is organized, reliable and structured, generally has a problem with the unstructured environment of large parts of the Internet (Landers and Lounsbury 2006), especially social-networking sites (Ryan and Xenos 2011). Agreeable personalities, those who are cooperative and trustful, are also found to be negative towards Internet use (Launders and Lounsbury 2006). Such individuals prefer face-to-face contact rather than the often antagonistic and conflictual relations in online discussion and networking. Finally, the evidence concerning neurotic personalities is mixed (Russo and Amnå 2016). Some researchers see that neuroticism hampers Internet use (Cullen and Morse 2011, observing online communities), while others note that it supports it (Correa et al. 2010, observing social media use).

In conclusion, openness to experience and extroversion certainly stimulate Internet use. Russo and Amnå (2016) conclude that, in the case of political communication, these traits support online political engagement.

We are now close to the end of the long list of causes of divides in digital media use, which are summarized in figure 6.2. The sequence of factors, apart from those pertaining to technical characteristics, is estimated. The remaining causes are a number of technical characteristics. Next to those affecting physical or material access and digital skills, there are also technical characteristics that influence the frequency, variety and type of digital media use.

Technical characteristics

A number of technical characteristics of contemporary digital media influence the resources people need to use these media. What are these characteristics? In the chapter on physical access we mentioned diversity. Some people have several different types of digital media while others may have only one device. In addition, devices have different potential usages, though the divide is mainly between smartphones or tablets on the one hand and desktops or laptops on the other. The former are not a full substitute for the latter. Smartphones and tablets have less memory, storage capacity and speed (Akiyoshi and Ono 2008; Mossberger et al. 2012; Napoli and Obar 2014) as well as a limited content availability (Napoli and Obar 2014), but they do offer more mobility (see below)

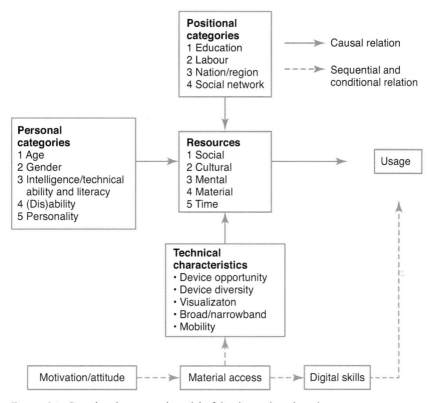

Figure 6.2. Causal and sequential model of divides in digital media use

and convenience and are cheaper in price. Smartphones, therefore, are frequently used for communication and entertainment (social networking and gaming) and when travelling, while desktops and laptops are often employed for information, education, business and work (Zillien and Hargittai 2009; Pearce and Rice 2013; Murphy et al. 2016). Thus people who own all these devices exhibit the most frequent and various digital media use. Van Deursen and van Dijk (2019) found in a representative survey in the Netherlands in 2018 that owning a greater range of devices is significantly related to a higher diversity of Internet use and a greater variety of outcomes.

A logical subsequent characteristic is *device opportunity*. Some devices offer wider opportunities for a more satisfying and diverse Internet experience (Donner et al. 2011). They can be combined with all kinds of peripheral equipment (van Deursen and van Dijk (2019); items can be printed, files can be scanned to be uploaded, large files can be saved on a hard drive, and larger screens can be added to multitask online and to show or present visuals. These functions are not possible with mobile devices. In the developed countries, many young people, some ethnic minorities, and those on low incomes tend to use just mobiles (Hargittai and Kim 2010; Tsetsi and Rains 2017), and this is the case for a large majority of Internet users in the developing countries. However, smartphones are not very satisfactory for information-intensive tasks such as online education, e-government and e-health services or for most professional applications. As a result some authors are already talking about a 'mobile underclass' and 'second class netizens' benefiting less from digital media (Napoli and Obar 2014, 2017; Mossberger et al. 2012).

A third technical characteristic is the availability of *broadband as compared to narrowband* Internet connections. Before broadband arrived in the 1990s, users had dial-up connections, which took a long time and were costly. With broadband they were liberated and motivated to spend more time on the Internet and for a growing number of applications. Today, some people prefer mobile connections to save the relative expense of broadband (Mossberger et al. 2012; Horrigan and Duggan 2015). In 2018, two-thirds of Americans had broadband at home while one in five had a smartphone only. Racial minorities, older adults, rural residents, and those with lower levels of education and income are less likely to have broadband service at home (Smith and Olmstead 2018).

The final characteristic affecting digital media use is the rise of *media with primarily visual content.* Social media such as YouTube, Instagram and Pinterest are becoming more and more popular. Television channels, video services and gaming are moving to the Internet. This trend favours those who are illiterate or intellectually disabled and stimulates people with low levels of education. However, because all complex tasks such as job applications use primarily *text media*, the divide between users with different levels of education is growing (for other reasons see below).

The consequences of divides in digital media use

Divides of digital media use and outcomes

The main consequence of the divides in digital media use is that the outcomes are also unequally distributed. In the next chapter we will see that this goes for both positive and negative outcomes. Those who are frequent and active users gain many benefits in the economic, social, cultural or political fields and in everyday living. They are also more capable when it comes to preventing negative outcomes such as cybercrime, bullying, insult or harassment, privacy infringement and loss of security.

The next general consequence is that all outcomes reinforce existing divides. Social resources will be strengthened, for example, by frequent, various and active social-networking use. Those who already enjoy social support will gain more, while the socially isolated will remain marginalized. Cultural resources – a conspicuous lifestyle, dispositions and status – are highlighted by active participation in digital culture. Mental resources will flourish in developing technical ability, cognitive and emotional intelligence, or digital literacy through frequent, various and skilful digital media use. Material resources may accumulate through good use of e-commerce, as products and services become cheaper. Employment can be found via online applications and professional networking. Finally, people will gain more temporal resources by means of efficient digital media use.

The usage gap

In the first decade of the twenty-first century, the age and gender distinctions were more pronounced in digital media use than social class and status (van Deursen and van Dijk 2014a). However, this is now changing rapidly, as we have seen that the older generations are catching up in Internet use. The same goes for gender and ethnic distinctions. In the meantime distinctions of social class or status, articulated primarily at the level of education and income, persist and tend to be increasingly important. This will be argued and demonstrated in the following chapters.

The term 'usage gap' was first used by van Dijk ([1999] 2012, 2000, 2004). Others described the phenomenon as the 'knowledge gap for the Internet' (Bonfadelli 2002), 'differentiated use' (DiMaggio at al. 2004), 'status-specific types of Internet usage' (Zillien and Hargittai 2009) or 'engagement in different Internet activities' (Pearce and Rice 2013). 'Usage gap' refers to a systematic use of the Internet for particular goals by people of higher social class (education, income and property) and status (social position and cultural resources) as compared to those of lower social class and status. The goals are advanced information, communication and education, work, business and capital-enhancing or career activities (higher social class) as opposed to simple information and communication (chatting or messaging), shopping and entertainment (lower social class).

The usage gap concept is inspired by the term *knowledge gap*, which was popular in the 1970s and 1980s. Tichenor et al. (1970: 159) stated that, 'as the diffusion of mass media information in a social system increases, segments of the population with a higher socio-economic status tend to acquire this information at a faster rate than the lower status segments.' However, the usage gap is broader and more consequential for society than the knowledge gap (which touches only on mental categories – learning – in using mass media), as it also refers to behaviour and activities in using the Internet and other digital media. The latter are multifunctional and are drawn on for all activities in society and daily life. The behavioural and systemic effects of the usage gap are much more important than the learning effects of the knowledge gap.

Since the year 2000 a usage gap in Internet activities has been demonstrated in a long series of studies. Van Dijk (2000: 177) predicted that the gap of simple and advanced types of political participation he observed among people of all classes and education levels will grow. Educated people contributed to online political discussion, became members of political organizations, ran as candidates and turned out to vote more often than those with lower levels of education, who tended only to sign online petitions and respond to Internet polls, and who didn't necessarily bother to vote. Bonfadelli (2002) showed that educated people used the Internet more actively and that their use was more information oriented, whereas the less educated seemed to be interested particularly in the entertainment functions of the Internet. DiMaggio et al. (2004: 39) assumed that higher-status users were more effective at converting access into information and information into occupational advantage or social influence than less privileged users. In the last ten years these observations have been confirmed by a growing number of studies, among them those by Hargittai and Hinnant (2008), Zillien and Hargittai (2009), Helsper and Galácz (2009), van Deursen and van Dijk (2014a), Pearce and Rice (2013), Buchi et al. (2016), Tsetsi and Rains (2017), Yates et al. (2015) and Yates and Lockley (2018).

The evolution of divides in digital media use

It is likely that the usage gap in social class and status will become wider in the future, while those of age, gender and ethnicity will become smaller but not disappear entirely; existing cultural preferences will most likely remain. This is because the gap is determined not only by socio-economic inequality but also by a cultural differentiation that is growing in postmodern society. Another reason for the expected growth of the gap in social class and status is the expected divide in digital and twenty-first-century skills, as discussed in chapter 5. People of higher social class and status have better skills in order to find advanced information and communication online for work, education and business than those of lower social class and status, who are more likely to explore consumption, communication and entertainment online.

Divides in digital media use are also the result of the general differentiation of social relationships, together with economic divisions of labour and culture in a postmodern network society. This increasingly individualized society consists of a large number of communities, organizations, cultures and ethnicities with different lifestyles and social or cultural preferences. The greater the diffusion of digital media in society and daily life, the more their use will vary. However, this is a general trend and not as specific as the usage gap of class and culture.

7   Outcomes

Introduction: who benefits and is harmed by digital media use?

After having described the causes and consequences of the phases of appro-priation of digital media, we have now arrived at the result of this process. What are the hazards of (not) using digital media? Does it matter if one has no access to the Internet, has insufficient digital skills and is an infrequent user, for example? It might be that traditional media remain adequate for many aspects of daily life, including work and education. We cannot rule out the fact that particular offline activities may be just as good as, or even better than, comparable online activities.

How can we understand these questions? Are they problems as far as economic growth, employment and innovation are concerned? Is there a problem of people being excluded from society and participation in all kinds of domains? Or is there a security problem because people cannot be easily registered and controlled by governments and businesses? These three perspectives were the main approaches of the digital divide as dis-cussed in chapter 1. In this chapter I am choosing the second perspective: inclusion in or exclusion from society. In my former book about the digital divide (van Dijk 2005) I took the normative perspective of participation in the labour market, the community, politics, citizenship, culture, etc. Here I am taking a more neutral and empirical approach: which positive and negative outcomes of digital media use have been observed? Up until now, digital divide research has been concerned with positive outcomes, out-comes achieved by people with digital access, skills and use. In this chapter, negative outcomes – excessive use, cybercrime or abuse, and loss of security or privacy – will be discussed. The question is what outcomes are achieved by people with an adequate level of access to digital media, together with the skills for their use.

The causal process behind the argument in this chapter is that fol-lowing the four phases of technology appropriation will lead to positive or negative outcomes. These outcomes then lead to the same resources causing the four phases of appropriation. This is a feedback loop of

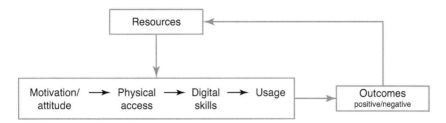

Figure 7.1. Causes and consequences of digital media appropriation for outcomes and the reinforcement of resources

reinforcement, a core statement of resources and appropriation theory as discussed in chapter 2. This particular statement is a case of structuration theory (Giddens 1984). In structuration theory, social structures influence actions, and actions affect these structures, a duality of reinforcement. In resources of appropriation theory, resources influence the process of appropriation, and the outcomes of this process reinforce the resources in a feedback loop. The argument is portrayed in figure 7.1. Supporting the resources are lists of both positional and personal categories as used previously. Via motivation/attitude, physical access, digital skills and usage, these categories will be related in this chapter to positive and negative outcomes.

The second section will frame the term 'outcomes'. These may be positive or negative, absolute or relative, concomitant or separate, online or offline, and traditional or digital media outcomes.

The third section is about the positive outcomes of digital media use. They are listed according to familiar domains of social and daily life: economic, social, cultural, political and personal. The most important potential outcomes for society and individuals will be discussed, related to positional and personal categories and added to a final score.

This is followed by the negative outcomes, which are clustered in three parts: excessive use, cybercrime or abuse, and loss of security or privacy. After this we will be able to see whether people who enjoy positive outcomes are also able to prevent negative outcomes.

The final section of this chapter draws up a balance sheet. What is the final situation with the digital divide? Considering all these positive and negative outcomes, are we able to conclude that the effects of digital inequality are increasing or decreasing? Which categories of society benefit more and are harmed less by the use of digital media? The answers are given in the following chapter, where digital inequality will be related to existing social inequality.

Framing the outcomes

The 'third level' of digital divide research (see chapter 1), which is a fairly recent focus, is to do with observing the outcomes. While the term was first used in 2010, empirical research of outcomes in terms of benefits started a few years later. Helsper and van Deursen (2015, 2017) undertook the most extensive surveys, in the UK and the Netherlands, showing the lack of equality in achieving benefits. Unfortunately, by that time the focus of most research was on positive outcomes. This is not surprising given that, from the start, all digital divide perspectives had focused on loss of economic growth, employment or innovation, the lack of participation or inclusion, and the failure to register or control citizens. After 2015 the general public became more aware of the negative consequences of the Internet, particularly in relation to social media, the rise of cyber-crime and all kinds of abuse, problems of disinformation, hacking, and excessive use.

Blank and Lutz (2018) were the first to investigate these negative outcomes. In their survey in the UK they asked participants whether they had experienced six specific harms: 'In the past year have you ever … received a virus onto your computer? … bought something which was misrepresented on a website? … been contacted by someone online asking you to provide bank details? … accidentally arrived at a pornographic website when looking for something else? … received obscene or abusive e-mails? … had your credit card details stolen?' While people on the right side of the digital divide clearly amassed the benefits of Internet use, the results concerning harms from using digital media were mixed for people on both sides of the divide. A similar conclusion will be drawn below after discussing a much longer list of negative outcomes.

A second type of framing is the estimation of outcomes. Are they absolute or relative? We will see that they are relative. Everybody who uses digital media experiences both positive and negative outcomes, some more than others.

Thirdly, outcomes may be observed separately and in combination. In this chapter we cluster them in linked domains of society For example, people gaining benefits from using social-networking sites might also discover more opportunities to find a job or a particular product in the economic domain. We will show that the economic and social domains and the cultural and personal domains are most closely related.

Finally, wherever possible, outcomes online have to be compared with similar offline outcomes. The same goes for digital and traditional media

use. What is the difference between finding a job online and doing so through using traditional media? An example of a question that might be asked here is: 'Without using the Internet, I would not have found a job. Yes/No'. In other words, a traditional job search would not have led to this positive outcome.

Positive outcomes of digital media use

Positive outcomes of digital media use are benefits generally endorsed by most contemporary societies. In the economic domain they are, for example, finding a job or lower prices for products or services. In the social domain they might be more and better contacts or relationships and contributions to the community. In the political and civic domain they might be voting in elections or receiving public and social benefits. In the cultural domain examples are attending, sharing or contributing to cultural events. In the personal domain they might be finding an educational course or benefiting from health information.

Table 7.1 lists the most important positive outcomes in all these domains that were part of nationwide Dutch and British surveys conducted by van Deursen and van Dijk (2012), Helsper et al. (2015), van Deursen and Helsper (2018) and Van Deursen (2018). Van Deursen and van Dijk (2012) and van Deursen (2018) posed questions such as 'By using the internet I obtained X: Yes/No'. Helsper et al. (2015) and van Deursen and Helsper (2018) asked not only for objective achievement but also for subjective satisfaction – for example, whether finding a romantic date online was satisfying. However, future survey questions need to become more valid and reliable, because answers may be biased and lack sufficient detail. So, one needs to be circumspect in accepting the data presented.

Economic domain

Positive outcomes in the economic domain for individuals are threefold and concern work and schooling, e-commerce (buying and selling online) and income or property. Digital media have become a necessity in most parts of the world as far as work and education are concerned. Both searching and applying for a job are now done mostly online, and those who lack the access or skills to do this are increasingly excluded from the labour market. Approximately three-quarters of Internet users who have found employment, at least in the UK and the Netherlands, claim that they have found a

Table 7.1. The most important positive outcomes of Internet use as achievements

Domain	By using the Internet I ...
Economic	– found a job opportunity
	– found a job
	– improved my work (tasks)
	– earned a higher wage
	– saved money buying a product or service online
	– saved money selling/sharing a product or service online
	– saved money investing in stocks or shares online
Social	– found friends I subsequently met offline
	– found a romantic date I subsequently met offline
	– have more contact with family, friends or acquaintances
	– have better contact with family, friends or acquaintances
	– found people sharing my interests
	– discovered an opinion online or added a new one
	– became a member of an association or community
Political/civic	– signed a petition online
	– contacted a representative, party or government department
	– became a donor of a political or civic organization
Political/civic	– became a member of a political or civic organization
	– voted after finding political information or using a voting aid
	– received better government information online
	– received a public or government service online
	– found a benefit, subsidy or tax advantage online
Cultural	– found a ticket online for an event or concert
	– found entertainment (games, music, video) not available offline
	– became a member of a hobby, sports or cultural club
	– changed lifestyle choices after receiving information online
	– created cultural content not available offline
Personal	– recognized my identity finding people with the same interests
	– found a course or study that fits me
	– completed a course or study outline
	– improved my health after finding health information online
	– found (more) about my disease
	– found a hospital or clinic to help me more quickly or to a greater degree

Source: Information from van Deursen and van Dijk (2012); Helsper et al. (2015); van Deursen and Helsper (2018).

job online they would not have found otherwise (van Deursen and van Dijk 2012; Helsper et al. 2015).

A majority affirm that they have found improvements in their job in terms of speed or productivity, through increasing flexibility and variety, and by receiving a greater number of courses (for using ICT) and more contacts with colleagues (van Deursen and van Dijk 2012). Finally, it has been confirmed from several sources that being able to use ICTs leads to a premium in wages (see chapter 5). All these positive employment outcomes have benefited the young (those aged sixteen to thirty-five) and people in the higher professions more than older (aged fifty-five plus) and non-professional workers (van Deursen and van Dijk 2012; van Deursen 2018).

Also in the economic domain is the market of products and services. For consumers – which means everybody – the advantages of e-commerce (buying and selling products and services) are among the most attractive benefits of Internet use. Large majorities assert that they have saved money buying a product online rather than in a shop and close to a majority that they have sold goods online that they wouldn't otherwise have sold. Again, young people and the higher educated benefit more (van Deursen and van Dijk 2012; Helsper et al. 2015; van Deursen 2018).

The third economic subdomain is property and income. A majority of people in the developed countries are now using Internet banking. The wealthy also are investing in stocks and shares. However, this minority need to have sufficient financial knowledge and a high level of information and strategic digital skills.

The conclusion here is that young people, particularly males, those with higher education or income, and the employed have statistically significant advantages of Internet use in this domain (van Deursen and Helsper 2018; van Deursen 2018).

Social domain

The use of digital media and especially the Internet offers many opportunities for social contact, civic engagement and sense of community; this was realised early on (e.g. Katz and Rice 2002; Quan-Haase et al. 2002), though some scholars doubted it (e.g. Nie and Erbring 2002; Putnam 2000). Twenty years on, the average American claims that helping people connect is the second best thing about the Internet after easier access to information (Pew Research Center 2018). Research involving nationwide surveys shows that a majority confirm they have found new friends online (and have subsequently met them in person) and that they also received more contacts (van Deursen and van Dijk 2012; Helsper et al. 2015). At least one-third of the Dutch population say that they have formed a better relationship with friends and family (van Deursen 2018).

Online dating is popular today and is becoming a real alternative to dating in traditional ways. More than 10 per cent of couples met online in the Western world (van Deursen and van Dijk 2012; Smith and Page 2016). The Internet is also helpful in finding people with the same interests or opinions, an activity performed by a majority of Internet users (see Helsper et al. 2015 for the UK). Finally, individuals can become members of associations or communities online, though this is realized by a relatively small minority of Internet users today (van Deursen and van Dijk 2012; Helsper et al. 2015; van Deursen 2018).

It would appear that these outcomes are achieved much more by young people than by older generations, although there is no significant difference in terms of level of education and income (van Deursen and Helsper 2018). This is because the use of social media is widespread and very popular.

Political and civic domain

Generally, there is more civic participation (using government services and engaging with local communities online) than political participation. Though in most countries a majority of people continue to go to the polls at election time, online political participation is a minority affair (Boulianne 2009; Anduiza et al. 2012; van Dijk and Hacker 2018). The most frequent activities are retrieving political and election information, discussing political affairs, mailing or messaging a political representative, and signing online petitions (Smith 2013). Nevertheless, a substantial minority in the UK secured a better contact with an MP, local councillor or political party (Helsper et al. 2015), while those in the Netherlands decided which party to vote for by using a voting aid (van Deursen and van Dijk 2012).

It would seem that people who are specifically interested in politics are benefiting most in this domain. Generally, such people are highly educated and have good incomes (Jorba and Bimber 2012; Smith 2013; van Dijk and Hacker 2018). The surprising finding is that it is older generations more than the young who are benefiting from online political applications (Smith 2013; Mounk 2018; van Dijk and Hacker 2018), probably on account of different motivations.

In developed countries, where people are increasingly forced to use online government services, there is a more widespread use of civic applications. However, we found the same inequality of access, skills and use as in most other domains: people with higher education or income and the young are benefiting most from more and better government information and services (van Dijk et al. 2008; United Nations 2014). Most telling is that a quarter to half of Dutch and British citizens claimed the discovery online that they were entitled to receive a particular benefit, subsidy or tax advantage that they would not otherwise have found (van Deursen and van Dijk 2012; Helsper et al. 2015; van Deursen 2018).

Cultural outcomes

Cultural use of the Internet is also very popular. Even novice users find music, video and games online that are not easily available elsewhere. Almost everyone has on occasion made an online reservation for an event. A much smaller majority of the Dutch and British population confirms that they have become a member of a hobby, sports or any other cultural club or that they changed their lifestyle after finding cultural information online (van Deursen and van Dijk 2012; Helsper et al. 2015; van Deursen 2018).

The number of people creating content online depends on the nature of that content: for example, 75 per cent of the British population have posted photos and shared them on social-networking sites, uploaded music and video, written a blog or set up a personal website. Creating skilled, professional-looking content was achieved by 34 per cent but political content only by 14 per cent (Blank 2013).

By far the most personal characteristic showing statistically significant differences in cultural outcomes is age, not level of education or gender (van Deursen and Helsper 2018), and young people manifest the greatest benefits in online cultural outcomes, even where skilled content creation is concerned. Social and entertainment content, however, is produced more by people of lower education (Blank 2013).

Personal outcomes

There are all kinds of personal benefits to be gained from using digital media or the Internet: two very important, even vital, benefits are personal development (identity and education) and health. A majority of Internet users manage to find people with the same interests, while a minority of British and Dutch users have found or completed a course of study online (Helsper et al. 2015). On the other hand, a majority of these users affirmed in 2012–15 that they had found details about their disease, improved their health after retrieving information, and secured better or faster health care after receiving advice online (Helsper et al. 2015).

Van Deursen and Helsper (2018) observed that people with a higher level of education achieve such personal outcomes more than do people with lower education. Remarkably, older generations are also benefiting more (especially where health and adult education are concerned) than the youngest generation.

Relations of domains and their outcomes

Helper (2012) claims that economic, social (including the political and civic domain), cultural and personal domains are interrelated. For example, someone who finds information concerning a job opportunity via a social-networking site may be able to secure the job in the economic domain. While the economic domain was generally found to be relatively separate, a strong link was found between social and cultural domain achievements in Dutch and British surveys (Helper et al. 2015). However, the most frequent interrelation found is between the personal and social and cultural domains (van Deursen and Helper 2018). The achievement of positive outcomes is found to be higher for economic and personal than for social and cultural outcomes (Helper et al. 2015). The online benefits in the economic and personal fields are higher than in the social and cultural field, where traditional media offer face-to-face alternatives.

Negative outcomes of digital media use

As previously mentioned, the negative outcomes of digital media use have become widely discussed in society only recently. They are the last focus in digital divide research (Blank and Lutz 2018). There are so many potential negative outcomes that it is difficult to classify and analyse them. Both a selection of experts and a representative sample of the American population found that the benefits of digital media for society and daily life were overwhelmingly positive (Pew Research Center 2018; Smith and Olmstead 2018). However, a small, albeit growing, number of experts and the general public were concerned about the negative outcomes. The experts mentioned mainly psychological characteristics: information and communication overload, problems of trust regarding security and privacy, especially in relation to the big Internet platforms, personal identity problems such as a loss of self-confidence or self-esteem, a negative world-view after using the Internet, and failures of concentration. The survey of ordinary Americans, also published by the Pew Research Center (Smith and Olmstead 2018), revealed the answers that the Internet 'isolates people' (25 per cent), produces 'fake news or misinformation' (16 per cent), is 'bad for children' (14

Table 7.2. The most important negative outcomes of Internet use as liabilities

Domain	Problems
Excessive use	– Addiction to the Internet and other digital media
	– Extreme stress in using the Internet and other digital media
	– Information overload
	– Loss of concentration
	– Lack of sleep
	– Lack of exercise
	– Lack of face-to-face communication
Cybercrime and abuse	– Financial fraud or theft
	– Extortion or blackmail (ransomware)
	– Identity theft
	– Criminal hacking of another's computer or connection
	– Bullying
	– Harassment
	– Provocation in Internet discussions (e.g. 'trolling')
	– Spam
	– Creation of disinformation
Loss of security and privacy	– All intrusion in a computer or smartphone
	– Data theft
	– Receipt of a computer virus or spyware/malware
	– No (attention to) privacy settings and agreements
	– Concerns about and inadequate use of passwords
	– No or inadequate computer protection: anti-virus programs, firewalls, automatic updates, spam-filters, pop-up blockers, anti-spyware

per cent), 'contains criminal activities' (13 per cent) and damages 'personal information or privacy' (5 per cent).

In this section I will deal with potential negative outcomes in three sections: excessive use, cybercrime or abuse, and loss of security or privacy (see table 7.2). These are individual negative outcomes rather than societal outcomes (for the latter, see, among others, van Dijk [1999] 2012). The discussion will relate these negative outcomes to the digital divide problem, looking at distinctions of age, gender, and social class and status (income, income and lifestyle).

To discuss these negative outcomes in a digital divide perspective we will look at the risks encountered by particular users and at the way they cope with these risks. People on the right side of the digital divide who are frequent users are more likely to encounter these risks; however, with their experience and skills they may also be better at coping with such risks.

Excessive use

Excessive use of digital media ranges from using a computer or the Internet for too many hours a day to outright addiction. Addiction is manifested in such activities as compulsive Internet shopping or gaming, or constantly checking Facebook, and results in withdrawal symptoms – mental and physical pain – when an individual tries to stop (Young 1998). In addition, other daily activities – work, school, sleep, exercise and eating – are impeded. Clearly, young people and those frequently using computers for work, education or leisure are liable to show excessive use. This is the flip-side of being included in the digital world.

Almost every research project concerning excessive use focuses on adolescents and young adults, who are most likely to take advantage of social-networking sites (SNS), messaging services and computer games. Excessive use of SNS is more of a problem for girls, while boys tend to play games too much (van Beuningen and Kloosterman 2018; Anderson et al. 2017). Excessive digital or social media use leads to a lack of concentration, e.g. at school and at work, as well as lack of sleep and face-to-face communication. In the Netherlands, 13 per cent of female Internet users consider themselves to be addicted to social media as compared to 7 per cent of males, though percentages among young people are generally higher (van Beuningen and Kloosterman 2018). However, as older generations make more use of SNS, messaging services and gaming, they too will exhibit such problems.

Excessive use is related more to mental characteristics and disorders such as (social) anxiety, depression and ADHD than to social characteristics of class, age and gender (Anderson et al. 2017). While particular users are more likely to be at risk in particular activities (SNS, chatting, gaming, gambling, etc.), some of them might also be better at coping with the problems. People with superior content-related digital skills, especially information, communication and strategic skills, and those with good social and parental relationships are more capable of reducing excessive use.

A related negative outcome is the problem of information or communication overload. Many people are overwhelmed by the amount and complexity of sources and messages on the Internet. In 2016, 20 per cent of American Internet users experienced information overload. Females, people above the age of fifty, and those with low incomes and an educational level of high school or less perceived significantly more information overload. They also had more trouble in coping with this problem (Horrigan 2016). Although there are no supporting data, it would seem most likely that individuals with good information, communication and strategic digital skills are better at handling these problems.

Cybercrime and abuse

It is possible for any Internet user to suffer from intrusion (hacking) and be a victim of computer identity theft (username and password). However, people with higher incomes and more property are also more likely to suffer from financial fraud or theft. However, the great majority of Internet users in the developed countries are now adopting Internet banking. In general, those with low education and incomes lack both the financial expertise and the digital skills (see chapter 5) to cope with such cybercrime.

The young users of social media and messaging services are more likely to encounter a number of other negative outcomes: bullying, unwanted sexting, harassment and provocation such as hate speech. While, in 2017, 41 per cent of Americans experienced some kind of Internet harassment (e.g. offensive name-calling, physical threats, racist comments, stalking and sexual harassment), younger people (aged eighteen to twenty-nine) suffered more than older generations (Duggan 2017). All kinds of harassment, with the exception of sexual harassment (Pew Id.), are more likely to be experienced by males than females. Neither social class nor education level were analysed in this Pew report.

A negative outcome that is receiving more attention of late is coming across disinformation on the Internet. This problem is encountered most by active information seekers. According to a survey published by the Pew Research Center, more than a third of American Internet users are engaged information seekers. Some of them are confident in using the Internet while others are eager to master its use better; they have much trust in particular information sources online (Olmstead and Smith 2017a). This section of the population is relatively young; the confident users have a high level of education and those eager to learn have a lower education and consist more of females than males. Other American users, those comparatively older – close to 50 per cent of the population – are wary about finding information online. They do not have much trust in information or news sources and have relatively low levels of information skills. They therefore will not recognize, or cannot cope with, disinformation when they come across it.

Coping with disinformation depends on trust in Internet sources and on one's information, communication and strategic digital skills. Only having sufficient skills will enable users to know whether or not to have confidence in a particular website. The same people who are confronted with (dis) information online, usually people with high levels of education, have more of these skills.

Loss of security and privacy

The more people use the Internet, the more they may be confronted with a loss of security, be it from hacking, data theft, or receiving viruses or malware. The same goes for loss of privacy through abuse of personal data or whereabouts. The knowledge and skills needed to prevent or repair such losses are unequally distributed. According to another survey published by the Pew Research Center, American Internet users were able to answer fewer than half the number of elementary questions asked about cybersecurity. Knowledge about such matters appeared to be much better among people with higher education and somewhat better among younger users (Olmstead and Smith 2017b).

The practice of preventing or repairing loss of security and privacy varies among people of different education and age. Those with higher education installed anti-virus programs, firewalls, automatic updates, spam-filters, pop-up blockers and anti-spyware more often than people with lower education. They also changed passwords more often and looked carefully at the addresses of e-mails they received (van Deursen and van Dijk 2012; Büchi et al. 2016).

The evidence pertaining to age and security or privacy is mixed. In 2011–12, van Deursen and van Dijk observed in Dutch surveys that the young (those aged sixteen to thirty-five) installed such protection less than older users. Users below the age of forty also tended to manage their privacy settings on Facebook less well (van den Broeck et al. 2015). However, in a Swiss survey, Büchi et al. (2016) found that older Internet users showed lower levels of privacy protection, mainly through a lack of 'Internet skills'.

What are the main conclusions about these negative outcomes of digital media use and the digital divide? Clearly, those who have access and the most frequent and varied use encounter these risks much more than others. However, many of them, especially the higher educated and the young, are also more competent in coping with them on account of having more Internet experience and better digital skills.

The balance sheet

We have seen that those on the right side of the digital divide of motivation, access, skills and usage are the ones who benefit more from the positive outcomes of digital media use in almost every domain. These are people with higher education and income, the young and, where particular applications are concerned, males. However, in some domains the situation is different: older users benefit more in political and personal domains (adult education and health applications); people with lower education and income benefit at least equally from SNSs in the social domain; and females benefit somewhat more from SNSs and personal development or health applications.

The flipside is that those on the right side of the digital divide are also the ones who have greater chance of encountering the negative outcomes of digital media. But, because they are generally more able to cope with the risks on account of having better digital skills, the result of experiencing negative outcomes is mixed.

The process of appropriation of digital media, as discussed in chapters 3 to 6, follows the model shown in figure 7.1 (see p. 97). Benefiting from positive outcomes *feeds back* to all resources. On the other hand, encountering and not coping sufficiently with the negative outcomes of digital media use *reduces* people's resources. For example, excessive use harms both one's mental resources (addiction, stress, overload, etc.) and one's social resources (less physical contact). People may lose money through cybercrime (material resources), be confronted with abuse (harassment and bullying) leading to loss of self-confidence, trust and status (mental, social and cultural resources). Digital skills and social or parental support are required to prevent such damage, but these are also unequally divided in society.

8   Social and Digital Inequality

Introduction: does digital inequality reduce or reinforce social inequality?

What is the relation between digital inequality and social inequality in general? This is the main question to be tackled in this chapter. When computers and the Internet arrived in the 1980s and 1990s, historical expectations were very positive and optimistic (examples are given in Naisbitt 1982; Rheingold 1993; Negroponte 1995; and Dyson 1997). The Internet would distribute knowledge and information in society easily, freely and cheaply. The educational opportunities were thought to be tremendous. The Internet would connect everybody far better than the telephone. People could find and create their own media content and not depend only on the mass media. Vertical hierarchies would be transformed into horizontal networks. Clearly, the dominant perspective was that digital media would reduce inequality and the scarcity of knowledge and information.

After the Internet bubble burst after the millennium, critical perspectives became more negative and pessimistic. One frame of reference was the problem of the digital divide. We have already seen that this problem is extremely complex and that it is unlikely to disappear.

The relation between digital media use and social inequality is suggested by the following three statements:

- digital media use reduces social inequality;
- digital media use makes no difference for social inequality;
- digital media use increases social inequality.

Actually, the word 'use' in these statements should read 'appropriation', following the sequence in this book – motivation, access, skills and usage – but 'use' sounds better. From the perspective of the digital divide, the third statement (increasing social inequality) seems obvious and is supported by the evidence and arguments of the previous chapters. However, we should not take it for granted. In chapter 7 we saw that there are both positive and negative outcomes of digital media use. Once the positive outcomes exceed the negative outcomes for every user, the result could be a reduction of social inequality in absolute terms: people formerly excluded from a particular domain could now be included. People with disabilities who are housebound can now receive services online.

I will now list some obvious arguments for all three statements. In the remainder of this chapter these relatively superficial arguments will be examined through more in-depth theoretical counter-arguments.

Digital media use reduces social inequality

There are a number of strong arguments to support the statement that digital media use reduces social inequality. A majority of people in the world are currently motivated and have a positive attitude towards digital media, which is quite a change from the situation in the 1980s and 1990s. In the developed countries, another majority of users now have physical access to digital media such as the Internet, and the developing countries are following suit. The most elementary operational and formal digital skills are being mastered by a large majority of users, and the frequency of use and the number of Internet applications has multiplied in the last fifteen years.

A second strong argument is that the enormous digital gaps in gender that were observed in the 1980s and 1990s have been closed in most parts of the world, while those in age are now reducing. The gap of levels of education has become less pronounced, although people of low education make different use of the Internet than people with higher education.

Chapter 7 showed that an overwhelming proportion of people are benefiting from the positive outcomes of Internet use in all important domains of society: economic, political-civic, social, cultural and personal. As a result, many would endorse the statement that the Internet, despite all criticisms, is a good thing for individuals and for society (as shown in the American survey by Smith and Olmstead 2018). Simultaneously, the negative outcomes are experienced primarily by those having best access and most frequent use of the digital media.

Another argument in support of digital media reducing social inequality is that, over time, all users benefit from the reduced costs of hardware, software and (some) services. Since the 1990s, the prices of computers, mobile phones and Internet connections have reduced considerably. The same goes for operational systems, office software and all kinds of smartphone apps. Internet provider services, music subscriptions and data bundles for mobile communication have also become cheaper, at least in terms of capacities offered.

The final argument is that using digital media offers low-cost and accessible information, most of which is paid for by advertising, so is free at the point of use. It is also more accessible than traditional sources; formerly, people had to go to a library, an agency or somewhere similar to find information, often in laborious ways. Today, Internet search engines are faster and much more intelligible.

Digital media use makes no difference for social inequality

The second statement, which observes digital inequality simply as *a reflection* of existing social inequality, also offers some strong arguments. The main one is that perceived inequalities are seen in traditional media use too. If someone has a literacy problem, it will handicap them in dealing with print media as well as with digital media. There are more similarities than differences between the two (see the balance in Van Dijk and van Deursen 2014).

A second argument is that people's basic personal and positional characteristics are the same in the digital and the offline world. Properties of age (stages of life) and gender are reflected everywhere. People with disabilities have problems in both worlds. Those lacking cognitive and emotional intelligence and technical ability meet problems in every context. Individuals with poor or low-paid jobs will not get a better job online and might end up with monotonous work such as data entry. Using digital media for schoolwork will not necessarily lead to better marks or a higher level of education. Poor living, working and schooling conditions in a developing country will be reproduced in the online world of that country.

Digital media use increases social inequality

The third statement argues that two types of inequality – absolute and relative – reinforce or increase existing social inequality. *Absolute inequality* means that people are excluded from or included in particular domains of society. When they are forced to use digital channels for which they have no access or skills, they will be excluded in absolute terms. They will not find a job without using the obligatory online job application; they will not be able to attend an event when all tickets are sold online; and they might not manage to obtain a particular social or public benefit without using online public or government services. While such functions are not yet universal in most countries, this is the trend. Increasingly, governments and businesses expect that people without the relevant access and skills can get support from others. In this way their position as second-class citizens, consumers and workers is further emphasized.

Relative inequality is more important for this third statement. This means that some people are participating in and benefiting *more or earlier than others* in all domains of society in the context of access, skills and use of digital media. Existing social inequality is reinforced because the material, mental, social, cultural and temporal resources of these individuals are improving while the resources of those without access and skills stay at the same level or are reduced.

A second set of arguments backing this statement claims that the problems in the four phases of technology appropriation are not dissipating; some are actually growing. Motivations and attitudes for digital media use have become more positive overall, but in chapter 3 we saw that large differences in motivation and attitude among users remain. Allegedly, physical access problems are disappearing in the developed countries, though material access problems and unequal possession of devices and connections remain (chapter 4). Inequality in digital skills, especially content-related skills, is growing as increasingly complex applications are offered (chapter 5). The frequency and diversity of digital media use is expanding, but diversity may lead to a structural and persistent gap between those using primarily capital-enhancing applications and those more interested in entertainment or less advanced communication and commerce (chapter 6).

The last set of arguments backing this statement concern the presumed declining costs and the level of accessibility in using digital media. It is questionable whether the prices for hardware, software and services are in fact declining. Adding all costs together, they might actually be increasing, though the investment compensates for the expense of other things now available online. For example, subscriptions for newspapers on the Internet are often cheaper than buying the printed versions. However, the numbers of devices, programs and subscriptions for digital media are multiplying. It is impossible to compile a full balance sheet of today's digital media household and business expenses.

Free online content is sometimes of low quality. Such content is paid for by often intrusive advertising and sometimes leads to a loss of privacy and security. The quality of online content is shrinking in this age of disinformation. Traditional media at least tried to provide news and information that was more or less reliable, while digital media provide both quality and poor sources of information and news. One of the risks concerning inequality is that, while some people are happy to pay for quality newspapers and information, others are satisfied with free news abstracts and low-quality information.

Clearly, there is more support in this book so far for the third statement than for the first two, despite the good arguments for these. So, to make my case, we have to dig deeper. The numerous demographics discussed in this book are too superficial. We need to look for more abstract concepts of stratification and social class to explain social and digital inequality. We should also pay attention to the changing societal and technological context.

These theoretical concepts will be discussed in the next section. Our societies are increasingly so-called information and network societies. In the information society, people lacking essential information are exposed to absolute inequality. In a network society, people in the best positions and with the best relationships benefit more. This means relative inequality.

We will then deal with the most important domains of social inequality: economic, social-network, cultural and personal. What are the trends in these domains without considering digital inequality? Is economic inequality rising in the world? We will link these domains of social inequality with the resources discussed in this book – material, mental, social, cultural and temporal resources – and then relate these domains to digital inequality.

In another section these separate domains of inequality will be combined as they are actually found in contemporary society. Nowadays people tend to live in separate worlds: they increasingly live, marry and have children with people of their own social standing. They reside in their own communities, homogeneous neighbourhoods and ghettos. In the digital world they locate themselves in 'hotspots', 'echo chambers' and 'filter bubbles'. Is segregation really happening in a network society that has the potential to connect everybody? If so, is digital inequality encouraging this?

I next sketch the evolution of the digital technology to come and what it means for the digital divide. So far we have dealt with 'simple' digital hardware, software and networks. The future is for the Internet of Things, artificial intelligence, big data and virtual or augmented reality. This technological complex will bring new challenges for digital media users. Some observers foresee a future of extreme inequality and an even wider digital divide.

The main questions of this book will be answered in the concluding section. Will the use of digital media reduce or reinforce social inequality, or does it make no difference? Is the digital divide here to stay or will it disappear?

114

Social inequality and digital divides

The context: the information and network society

To understand the workings of the digital divides discussed in this book we have to consider some basic characteristics of contemporary society. Although these abstract characteristics are very important, they are not reflected and discussed in the theory and model of the resources and appropriation theory framing this book. First, we are now living in a society in which the production of information seems to have become even more important than the production of material goods. Data comprise the raw material of information, while information is an interpretation of data. An information society is a society in which the information intensity of all activities has become extremely high (van Dijk 2005: 134).

In the information society, information is both a primary and a positional good or asset. *Primary goods* are so essential for survival and self-respect that they cannot be exchanged for other goods (Sen 1985). They are not only the means of sustaining life, or life chances, particular rights and freedoms, but they also serve as basic information for individuals to survive in society. Primary goods of information are expressed by the *basic knowledge of how our complex society works*: the markets of labour and exchange, housing, transport, education and health care. In an information society, those who are completely illiterate are not able to live without help.

Having or lacking primary goods means *absolute* (in)equality. The relationship with the digital divide here is that, when essential information for living in a particular society moves online, primary goods of information can be lost for those without digital access or skills. Meanwhile, the quality and ease of use of essential information offline may become less good. For example, it might be that a systematic comparison of the best hospital for the treatment you need can be found more easily on a health care site than by consulting your doctor.

Positional goods are goods that people value because of their limited supply and because they convey a high relative standing within society. Thus information as a positional good means that *particular information is not readily available to all*. Some people in society and the economy have more opportunity of accessing this information than others (Hirsch 1976). Teleworking at home has not made a breakthrough in society partly because some crucial information is still obtained by talking to colleagues in the workplace, if only during a coffee break. A clear example of a positional good is the prior knowledge of insider traders: those who work in an investment company are in a better position to make decisions on the stock market than outsiders. Despite the move towards information being online, offline positions remain decisive when scarce or unique information is required.

Lacking positional goods means *relative* (in)equality, and such goods are becoming more important in the information society. They also mark the digital divides of skills and usage. For example, there are work roles that involve a range of tasks, from entering data in spreadsheets and databases through designing and applying decision support systems with artificial intelligence. The latter tasks define the data and the information to be used and the former simply apply it.

However, the most important reason why information as a positional good is becoming more important is because the information society has also become a *network society* (van Dijk [1991] 2001, [1999] 2012; Castells 1996; Barney 2004). The infrastructure of a modern network society has social and media networks at every level: individual, group/organizational and societal (van Dijk [1991] 2001, [1999] 2012). This can be compared to a *mass society* (a society with an infrastructure of 'masses' – organic groups, organizations and communities in which people are living). In an individualized network society, an individual has to be strong to acquire and keep their position; in a mass society an individual can be taken along by the group or community ('mass') to which they belong. The network society tends to become more unequal than the mass society (van Dijk [1999] 2012).

The network society is marked by relative inequality because the positions and relations in its social and media networks are distributed unequally. This is the case both for offline social networks and for online media networks, the focus of this book. Traditional social networks and new digital media networks are integrated, and in this way positions of social networks are reflected and reinforced by positions in digital media networks. When social and media links are combined, the strength of their links will be different, leading to a structure of power in a tripartite society (see figure 8.1).

In the network society you have an 'information elite' – a minority of units or people with strong social and media network relations. They have the best access opportunities and skills and the most frequent and varied digital media use, while the majority of the population, even in the developed countries, enjoy lesser social and media network relations. Access, skills and usage are also more limited. Finally, the unconnected and excluded from the network society have only traditional social network relations which, in turn, are less frequent and dense than those of the majority.

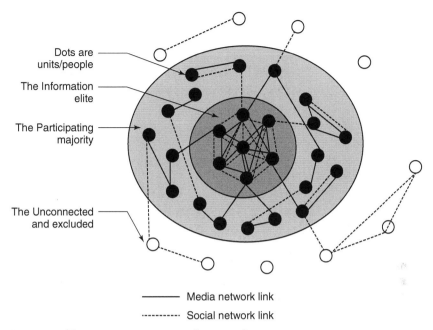

Figure 8.1. Tripartite participation in the network society
Source: Van Dijk (2005: 179).

The positions, links and resources of the information elite tend to become stronger than the positions, links and resources of the majority in the network society. This is a case of the so-called Matthew effect (Merton 1968) – the name comes from the Gospel of St Matthew (13: 12): 'For whosoever hath, to him shall be given, and he shall have more abundance.' The popular adage is 'the rich are getting richer'. The scientific backing for this trend is the statistical regularity of the power law, which says that a relative change in one quantity results in a proportional relative change in another; in this context, then, a few units of a network already having many links acquire even more, while most units retain only a few links.

Social classes and digital divides

The positional categories of labour, education and social-networking connections and their contexts in nations/regions and households have already been described in the previous chapters. In fact they are clustered in social classes. This is an important analytic distinction in social science, part of stratification theory that attempts to explain the social strata of society. There are many concepts and theories of social class, but most of them come from the classical Marxian or Weberian tradition or from modern sociology, with scholars ranging from critical sociology (Bourdieu) to mainstream sociology (Goldthorpe). See the summaries of class approaches in Wright (2005). The Marxian tradition (summarized in Draper 1978) looks mainly at the positions of production relations: capital versus labour. Weber ([1922] 1978) focuses on market relations and the life chances of individuals, while Bourdieu (1987) distinguished various kinds of capital as resources: economic, social and cultural. Finally, mainstream sociology (e.g. Goldthorpe et al. 1987) analysed primarily labour market positions with occupations and status.

In this book I will try to merge these concepts in a general image and analysis of social class in order to relate this broadly to the digital divide. I have maintained the popular distinction of upper class, middle class and working class. To differentiate this distinction further, traditional and new middle and working classes are introduced. The new middle class of professionals and the new working class of flexible service workers are the fastest growing social classes in contemporary society, while the traditional middle classes and working classes are shrinking. Finally, an underclass, or precariat, is added to the spectrum (Standing 2011). Members of this class have the lowest paid and most insecure jobs; they might also be permanently unemployed and/or have no home.

My distinction comprises six social classes merging the social class perspectives of Marx, Weber, Bourdieu and Goldthorpe. They are the *upper class* (the bourgeoisie, capitalists or the old elite), the *new middle class* (the new professionals or the new elite), the *traditional middle class* of shopkeepers, farmers, doctors and teachers, the *traditional working class* of industrial, construction, transportation and care workers, the *new working class* of flexible service workers, more or less skilled and largely doing manual work, and, finally, the *underclass or precariat*. This six-class distinction is a combination of economic classes such as the bourgeoisie, the working class and independent farmers or shopkeepers (Marx), status distinctions of 'up', 'middle' and 'under' or 'elite' (Weber and Bourdieu's cultural capital) and occupations such as industrial or service workers and teachers (Goldthorpe).

In the developed countries roughly *less* than one-third of the population is part of the upper class and the new middle class, one-third belongs to the traditional middle and working class, and *more* than one-third comprises the new working class and the underclass. In developing countries the traditional middle class (farmers and shopkeepers, often poor), together with the traditional working class and the underclass, is still much larger than that in developed countries. The characteristics of these six classes are stratified according to high, medium and low levels (see table 8.1).

Table 8.1. Estimated levels of characteristics of social classes in developed countries

Characteristics Social class	Property	Income	Labour position	Education	Social network contacts	Cultural capital/ preference	Digital access	Digital skills
Upper class (the bourgeoisie, old elite)	High	High	High	High	High	Classical	High	Medium
New middle class (new professionals, new elite)	Medium	High	High	High	High	Classical/ popular	High	High
Traditional middle class (e.g. shopkeepers, doctors, teachers, farmers)	Medium	Medium	Medium	High/ medium	High/ medium	Classical/ popular	High	Medium
Traditional working class (e.g. industrial workers, construction workers, care or transportation workers)	Low	Medium	Medium/ low	Medium/ low	Medium/ low	Popular	Medium	Medium
New working class (flexible service workers)	Low	Low	Low	Medium/ low	Medium/ low	Popular	Medium/ low	Medium/ low
Precariat/underclass (e.g. cleaners, cashiers, catering workers, homeless or regularly unemployed people)	Low	Low	Low	Low	Low	Popular	Low	Low

The usual characteristics of social class (property, income, labour position, education and forms of capital or life chances) are compared to the characteristics of digital access and digital skills as discussed in this book. When the estimations are justified, the parallel of social and digital inequality is striking. The upper class and the new middle class have the best digital access and skills. The new working class and the underclass have low levels of access and skills. The traditional middle class and working class show medium levels of digital access and skills. This distribution is supported by the survey data discussed in the earlier chapters under the characteristics of digital media (non-)users: income, education and labour position together with social and cultural capital.

The distribution conforms with similar social class comparisons inspiring my scheme – the Great British Class Survey organized by the BBC (Savage et al. 2013: 230) and a Dutch survey (Boelhouwer et al. 2014: 292) – though their class labels are different. The result is also similar to the comparison of social class and digital media use by Yates et al. (2015), although these authors used the UK National Readership Survey classification of social grade (based primarily on occupations). Their survey also found that, as far as the Internet was concerned, the lowest social classes (skilled, semi-skilled and unskilled manual workers, casual and lowest grade workers, and people living on social benefits or pensions) revealed low and limited use, less varied use, and less information-seeking behaviour. However, these classes were much more frequent users of social media (see also Yates and Lockley 2018).

To lend more support to this distribution, I will now briefly summarize the current trends of inequality in the most important domains of society and relate these trends to digital inequality.

Economic inequality

Most economists agree that economic inequality has increased in almost every part of the world in the last thirty to forty years. Although fast-growing emerging economies such as China, India and Brazil have created a relatively wealthy middle class and the prosperity of the whole population has increased, relative inequality inside these economies has also grown (Milanovic 2016). The range between the very rich and the very poor in China is now much larger than during Mao's time (Shambaugh 2016). Both absolute and relative inequality have increased in the Western developed countries, where the incomes of the lowest classes (the traditional and new working class and the underclass), taking inflation into account, have in fact remained at much the same level for forty years. Recently the incomes of the middle class have also fallen; all productivity growth has gone to the upper class (Stiglitz 2013), mostly as a result of their steep accumulation of property or capital (Piketty 2014).

One of the reasons why the majority of the population, at least in the developed world, could not afford to acquire what were then relatively expensive computers and Internet connections in the 1980s and 1990s was because the level of their income and property had stagnated. Only once prices had gone down and digital media had become a necessity did access and use multiply fast. However, inequality of material access is still a problem even in the richest countries (see chapter 4). In the developing countries, the cost of all digital media is still so high that access and use remain a problem.

People with high levels of economic capital (income and property), and mostly also highly educated and having a professional career or a modern business, benefit more from the positive economic outcomes of digital media use (see chapter 7). They are part of the upper class of capital owners or the new middle class of professionals who gain the advantages of cheaper consumer goods and services (Helsper et al. 2015; van Deursen and Helsper 2018) and through acquiring capital goods and services. Because members of the upper class have not only capital but also the advanced financial and digital skills – sometimes hired – necessary to buy and sell on the world's stock exchanges and financial markets, they manage to accumulate capital (Piketty 2014). The upper and new middle class also profit from employment relations online (Helsper et al. 2015): for them, a specialized social-networking site such as LinkedIn is much more powerful than a general one such as Facebook, so popular among the rest of society.

Clearly, digital inequality reinforces relative inequality in the economic domain. For the social classes at the highest end of the spectrum, use of digital media is literally capital-enhancing.

Social network inequality

The total volume of social capital (the number of social contacts) in contemporary society is expanding overall. This is a consequence of a network society with growing individualization and mobility and where people live, work and spend leisure time separately (van Dijk [1999] 2012). The Internet, and especially social media, has given a boost to new and existing relationships (Ellison et al. 2011; Wang and Wellman 2010; Rainie and

Wellman 2012; Poushter et al. 2018). The quality of such relationships with friends, colleagues and acquaintances is another matter, however, as some of them have become less intensive or complex and more diluted or superficial (Mesch and Talmud 2011).

However, the distribution of this growing social capital has also become more relatively unequal. People with high incomes or education and a higher profession – in general, the upper and new middle class – have a much larger network than people with low income or education and lower occupations – in general, the traditional and new working class and the underclass (see Poushter et al. 2018 for the US, Savage et al. 2013 in the UK, and Boelhouwer et al. 2014 for the Netherlands). See also the assumptions of table 8.1 and figure 8.1. The disparity is not so much among core or strong ties (family and friends) as among significant weak ties (colleagues, acquaintances, customers and contacts online whom one never meets in person).

Significant weak ties matter in a network society, as Granovetter (1983) explained in his article 'The strength of weak ties'. They offer valuable resources which are not found by people with fewer weak ties. In general, social networks provide access to valuable resources (Tilly 1998; DiMaggio and Garip 2012). Networks show *network effects* that exacerbate inequality in the adoption of beneficial practices (the positive outcomes of chapter 7). Network effects are of three kinds: network externalities, social learning and normative influence (DiMaggio and Garip 2012). With network externalities, the early members of a network profit both first and the most when others join in; with social learning, the larger your network, the more support you can obtain and the more you can learn from others; and, with normative influence, the larger your network, the more contacts you have available to ask for advice before taking decisions.

These network effects can also be related to social class. Tilly (1998: 10) has explained that powerful, connected people command resources from which they draw significant returns by *exploiting* outsiders who have been excluded from the full value of the network. These powerful connected people are *hoarding opportunities* in the network because they have greater access to resources that are valuable, renewable and a subject of monopoly and social support.

The rise of digital media has reinforced the unequal distribution of social capital and all these network effects. The results are the unequal social resources discussed as causes for all four phases of the digital divide: motivation, physical access, digital skills and usage.

Cultural inequality

Just as in the economic domain growth occurs worldwide and in the social domain the number of contacts increases, in the cultural domain cultural production and consumption are rising. This is a side effect of the growing diversity in postmodern society (see chapter 6). Inequality exists in the cultural domain, though it is less visible, since diversity, rather than exclusion, has become the principle of cultural distinction today (Ferrant 2018). In the past, those in the higher social classes distinguished themselves through 'high-brow' culture, in comparison to the masses, with their popular, 'low-brow' culture (Bourdieu [1979] 2010).

Today, *all social classes* have become *omnivorous* in creating and consuming culture (Peterson 1992), so that 'even the snobbiest of snobs' (Coulangeon 2015) among the upper and middle classes enjoy popular culture (Ferrant 2018). However, the distinction is not that some classes are more omnivorous than others (Warde et al. 2007) but that some types of culture are peculiar to specific classes. While the upper and middle classes frequently enjoy classical music, art and literature, a large proportion of the working and underclasses show little interest in such matters but prefer popular music or literature, videos, TV programmes and games or watching sports.

Surveys in the UK (Bennett et al. 2009; Savage et al. 2013) have shown that the higher classes appreciate both classical and popular culture, while the lower classes focus more on popular culture (see also table 8.1). This is reflected in digital media use, where the higher classes benefit from all kinds of online culture, while the lower classes limit themselves to video, television, film, pictures, music, sports and games. Witte and Mannon (2010: 114) conclude, in analysing American surveys, that 'the intensive and extensive nature of Internet use among the well-off and well-educated suggests an elite lifestyle from which the poor and uneducated are marginalized.'

Inequality of personal development

The personal domain has become the principal domain of life for individuals in a late-modern or postmodern society. According to Giddens (1991), this importance is revealed in the rise of self-identity as a 'reflective project'. Whereas, before modernity, certain decisions were made largely by the community and the family, individuals are now constantly confronted with lifestyle choices, whether in the field of food, health, education, work, leisure, social and family relationships, children or their own personal well-being.

Digital media are very powerful tools to support these areas. Increasingly, people are looking on the Internet to find lifestyle and leisure choices or options, to discover what disease they think they have and its treatment, and to search out food choices and recipes. They are also looking for support to realize their potential, for life coaching and even to overcome loneliness. And they may search for training courses or other kinds of adult education.

The story here is much the same: the personal domain is growing, but so is the inequality in benefits. The opportunities for personal development via the Internet are being taken mostly by people with higher education and incomes and, for some activities, also young people (working on self-identity and spending leisure time) and females (health and food information). See a number of benefits combined in Helsper et al. (2015) and Helsper and van Deursen (2017). Those who are in greatest need of the key benefit, health information and care, are the elderly or disabled and people with low education, who on average have more health problems; but *they are using these applications less* (see van Deursen and van Dijk 2012; Hale 2013; Robinson et al. 2015). According to a Pew health online report (Fox and Duggan 2013), at that time Americans with college grades used them roughly double more than Americans with high school grades, and young people (age 18–29) more than the elderly (65+), although the information retrieved spurred them equally often to go to a doctor.

A balance sheet

Taking into account these four domains, the conclusion is evident: today digital inequality not only reflects but also tends to reinforce social inequality. Digital media are powerful tools that support people who already have an advantage in a particular domain, while those who are already disadvantaged in certain respects benefit less. The parallel between the social and the digital media characteristics of social class summarized in table 8.1 is striking. In the future, the use and the benefits of digital media may become more equally divided in *absolute* terms. The question is whether *relative* inequality will also be reduced.

Separate worlds: the trend of segmentation

So far we have looked at domains of society or life and people's individual resources, combining them only in the general concept of social class. In fact these domains and resources are related in many ways. Helsper (2012)

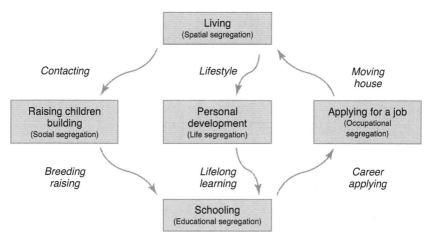

Figure 8.2. A cycle of segregation in various life domains

talks about corresponding fields, and van Deursen et al. (2017) discuss compounded inequality. People are divided not only by social class but also by ethnic, cultural, health (ability), age and gender distinctions; these may be conceived as *stratification* (high and low) in terms of hierarchy and as *segmentation* in terms of distance (separation). Social segmentation of society is a strong term, but in fact we can see social categories drifting apart in all domains of society (Bruch and Mare 2008). While there has been much investigation of residential, ethnic, school and occupational segmentation, all domains of life and society are affected, often by the even stronger process of *segregation* (structurally living and working apart). Figure 8.2 depicts the links between these domains and shows cycles in which people move from segregation in one domain to similar segregation in another domain. This figure was designed to describe what this means for the digital divide.

While in earlier societies segmentation was derived by birth or descent, in modern society it is achieved by property, work, education and lifestyle. Late-modern or postmodern society created even more distinctions of a cultural kind (Turner 1990; Giddens 1991). Today, the network society links all sorts of abstract social segments or concrete small worlds with strong ties to the rest of society via weak ties (Milgram 1967; van Dijk [1999] 2012). All these distinctions are marked by particular differential resources and types of inequality.

The most important of these distinctions and inequalities today are the divides of social class, especially the level of education, as they characterize all domains of society and life. Starting with the domain of 'living' in figure 8.2, we find, on the one hand, people with low education in neighbourhoods that are predominantly poor and, on the other, those who are more highly educated in well-off areas. Today there is a trend of residential segregation in large parts of the world, as the social mix between people is declining (Ostendorf et al. 2001). This applies especially to the poor, who tend to congregate in neighbourhoods with others of similar background (Volker et al. 2014; Hofstra et al. 2017). Moving anticlockwise in figure 8.2, most people start a family and raise children from within their own communities. These children then go to schools in their own neighbourhoods with other children of the same class or ethnic composition, a process of school segregation.

When leaving school and applying for a job, these children of mostly working-class and underclass families are more likely to find employment at a similar level to that of their parents than a job at another, perhaps higher level (occupational segmentation). Later, these children find a home in the same or a similar neighbourhood. In all these domains they will reproduce the same, sometimes unhealthy lifestyle, with such problems as obesity and heart disease, and a low level of lifelong learning in adult education.

This is an extreme picture of segregation with no upward social mobility. At the other extreme we find high or persisting social mobility among upper-class and middle-class people, starting with the domain of work. It is here, and in their friendship network, rather than in the neighbourhood, that such people meet their contacts (Volker et al. 2014). Most likely they will find a partner of the same social class and level of education. They will reproduce their culture in bringing up their children, who will attend good schools (not necessarily in the neighbourhood) with the same kind of children. These children will most likely secure employment away from home, probably in an urban environment, at a level similar to that of their parents. They will move wherever is necessary in order to support their career. They are more likely to have a relatively healthy lifestyle and all kinds of choices and lifelong learning options.

The majority of people worldwide fall between these two extremes, as segmentation never reaches 100 per cent. However, many present-day sociologists are concerned about the rise of social segmentation and the creation of separate lives accompanying these societal divisions (Coleman 1990; Wrzus et al. 2013; Musterd et al. 2017). They also argue that upward social mobility, so clearly observed since the mid-twentieth century with the rise of higher education, is now stagnating or even declining. Some see polarization between the extremes highlighted above (Gaschet and Gallo 2005; Vuyk 2017).

This has been a long introduction to the main proposition of this section, which is that the use of digital media reflects and reinforces these segmentation processes more than it reduces them. To understand this, one needs to appreciate two main opposing characteristics of digital media networks: they are able to *connect* everybody in society and they are able to *select* favoured others (van Dijk [1991] 2001, [1999] 2012) – heterogeneity versus homogeneity. However, in practice, the temptations of selection and homogeneity are dominant because people want to have their views confirmed (against cognitive dissonance; Festinger 1954) and tend to move towards the familiar and to stay in their own group (homogeneity and groupthink; see Sunstein 2008).

In digital media use, *selection* is the main mechanism supporting the social segregation tendencies discussed in at least four network activities: 1) contacting, 2) producing, consuming and sharing resources, 3) choosing places to live, work and go to school and 4) exchanging opinions. One aspect of contacting is online dating. In most countries today there are popular online dating sites aimed only at people with higher education (Skopek et al. 2010). Clearly, this supports social segregation where relationships and family-building are concerned. Having good connections in social-networking sites (a social resource) might lead to new job opportunities (an economic resource). There are also many Internet applications for fine-tuning job selection, finding a course of study, and selecting a place to live. Finally it is easy on the Internet to exchange opinions with people of the same interests and views, a process that is often described pejoratively as visiting 'echo chambers' and being stuck in 'filter bubbles' (Sunstein 2001; Pariser 2011).

However, just as segregation is never total, people do not only search for and exchange views similar to their own (van Dijk and Hacker 2018). They also browse through unexpected sites and are accidentally exposed to new sources, people they do not know, and opposing views (Brundidge 2010; Lee et al. 2014; Barberá 2015). Deliberately seeking reinforcement of one's views is the action of a minority (Karlsen et al. 2017).

Intentionally looking for quality information and news online, and paying for the privilege, is an activity undertaken primarily by a minority of people with higher education and income. The majority is tempted to use free news and information sources, often of lower quality. This will be one of the most important manifestations of the digital divide in the future (van Dijk and Hacker 2018).

The evolution of digital technology and inequality

Basic changes are taking place in digital media technology, all of which are capable of increasing or reducing social inequality. Four major directions will change the relations between humans and digital media.

The first direction is the *multiplication* of digital media. Alongside a growing number of computer types, most traditional media – televisions, cameras and audio equipment – are being manufactured in digital form. There are new types of digital media: wearables, all kinds of meters, virtual and augmented reality devices, and many others. These devices are cheaper than traditional media, and the skills needed to operate them are similar (the same kind of menu operations), thus offering the potential to reduce the digital divide. However, the disadvantages are that all these devices together probably cost more than all the former traditional media combined and that people may have to learn several different operating systems. The multiplication of digital media also means that the process of appropriation recurs several times.

The second direction is the most basic. Up to now, digital divide research has dealt with the 'simple' dual interface of humans and devices or connections driven by software – human–computer or human–media interaction. We are now in an era where people work not only with interfaces of hardware and software but also with *interfaces of systems*. The digital media of the Internet of Things, for instance, are coordinated by systems. Examples are the system for advanced home energy meters and the system of health providers offering patients meters for heart conditions and diabetes or for coaching healthy people with wearables for exercise or sport. Another example is the transport system for safety cars steered by sensors and for self-driving cars.

Users need to know how these systems work and for whom they are providing their data. This is a big problem. Most users – perhaps only 1 or 2 per cent of the entire population on earth – do not even know how the Internet as a system works, and the complicated systems just mentioned are even more difficult to understand and be controlled by the average user. A high level of content-related digital skills, which most people do not have, is required to use the applications of the Internet of Things, where 'more emphasis [will be] on information skills (selection, interpretation, and quality assessment), communication skills (understanding how devices communicate with other devices and humans and vice versa, and how users communicate with other users in the IoT system), and strategic skills (deciding what data should be collected and how it should be used to gain optimal outcomes)' (van Deursen and Mossberger 2018: 131).

These new digital media are directed by artificial intelligence and continually produce big data. Decisions are made not only by users but also automatically by algorithms, so users need to have the strategic skills to follow or overrule these decisions. However, most often people are not informed about the working of these algorithms; nor is it clear who possesses the data and the algorithms processing them – the user, the IoT provider or the system and organizations concerned. If these conditions prevail, the Internet of Things and any other digital media directed by AI and big data will considerably enhance digital and social inequality.

Those individuals who were the first to adopt and use the older digital media, computers and the Internet have also been the first to adopt these new digital media. In a survey in the Netherlands in 2018, people with higher education used the applications of the Internet of Things roughly twice as much as people with lower education. Similarly, young people were far more frequent users than older people (van Deursen et al. 2018).

The third technical direction in the evolution of digital media is *miniaturization*, which encompasses both *external* hardware, such as wearables, and implanted devices or chips, where individuals become cyborgs. Here technology becomes quite intimate and may make people more powerful. Smart devices can also boost our intelligence.

The popular historian Y. N. Harari (2016, 2018) has a vision of the future in which super humans are created alongside normal humans. The super humans are the information elite, with not only the best digital skills but also the power to afford, to deal with and to control advanced data worn on or as implants in the body. Normal humans would become superfluous or irrelevant once most jobs are fully or largely automated and robotized. Harari envisages a future of extreme inequality. His pitch-black dystopian vision unfortunately is not some kind of science fiction, and according to my analysis a milder version may become reality. An ever more powerful information elite, consisting of upper-class people and the professional new middle class, with full possession of digital technology and high information and strategic twenty-first-century skills, distancing itself from the rest of the population is not an impossible future.

The fourth direction is *the integration or merger* of computers and the online world with physical reality and the offline world. This is being realized by the applications of virtual, augmented and mixed reality (mixed reality: an example is a holograph projected on a physical scene). Today these are used in the entertainment, health care and educational sectors. The equipment is rather expensive at present. Moreover, the interfaces are complex, so people need special operational and cognitive skills, as well as high information, communication and strategic skills, to understand and cope with these new applications. As ever, it is people with higher education and incomes and the young who have been the early adopters of this technology.

These four directions are new challenges for society, and all tend to intensify the digital divide and social inequality.

Conclusions

The major conclusion of this chapter is that digital inequality, or the digital divide, tends to reflect and reinforce existing social inequality. This is first of all a matter of relative inequality. Some people and some social classes benefit more and earlier from the outcomes of digital media use than others. Relative inequality matters in a network society where some are able to take greater advantage of resources via relationships than others. In terms of absolute inequality, digital media use may reflect and reinforce existing social inequality when the positive outcomes are reached only by some in society. Absolute inequality matters too in an information society when some cannot find vital information necessary to live and work. When the use of digital media becomes absolutely essential, those without access or elementary digital skills will be excluded.

We have seen that use of digital media makes a difference as far as existing social inequality is concerned. There is a wide *spectrum* between those who do not use digital media at all and have no skills and those who use it frequently and have superior skills; this range is now *wider and more diverse* than was that between the unlettered and intellectuals in the past. Similarly, the illiterates did not possess and were not able to use traditional press media while the intellectuals used them frequently and with high skill. Nowadays it is not only a matter of literacy, it is also to do with taking action online (see chapter 6).

Furthermore, today digital media are *everywhere*, in all spheres of life. Traditional media were concentrated in particular in schools and some workplaces and were important for leisure pursuits. Thus I have argued that the gap in digital media use is more important than the knowledge gap in traditional media. People draw on digital media for much more than just deriving knowledge.

The reflection and reinforcement of digital inequality in existing social inequality is intensified when we look at the background of social class (see table 8.1). The characteristics of digital media are able to reflect and reinforce the characteristics of social class. If these characteristics accumulate in all domains of living, these social classes are going to live in separate worlds.

Regarding the evolution of new digital technologies such as the Internet of Things, decision apps based on artificial intelligence, and virtual or augmented reality, we have seen that there is a greater chance that digital divides and social inequality will increase. This new technology might be easier to operate because more and more decisions are made automatically, but satisfactory use and real benefit might be more difficult to achieve than is the case with older digital technology. Advanced content-related and twenty-first-century digital skills, and at least some knowledge of artificial intelligence and data processing, are required.

The digital divide is here to stay. We have seen that motivation or attitude and physical access have improved, but that the gaps in digital skills and usage are only increasing. At the same time, motivation/attitude and physical access divides have not been closed completely, and certainly not in the developing countries.

Perhaps the most important and evident conclusion of this book is that it is impossible to close the digital divide without reducing other social inequalities. Focusing merely on the problem of the digital divide will lead only to its mitigation. However, the best solution would be to reduce existing social inequality and digital inequality simultaneously. We will now turn to this idea in the final chapter.

9   Solutions to Mitigate the Digital Divide

Introduction: can the digital divide problem be solved or only mitigated?

One of the most important conclusions of this book is that the digital divide cannot be closed without reducing existing social inequalities. I have argued here that it is the unequal material, mental, social, cultural and temporal resources of people that are its causes. While digital media use can show positive outcomes and potentially lead to less inequality, currently the regular use of these media actually reflects and reinforces existing inequalities. This is not the fault of the digital media themselves. At a time when social inequality was decreasing, as was the case in many countries for about thirty years after the Second World War, digital media might have contributed to the *reduction* of social inequality.

Unfortunately today, most existing economic, social and cultural inequalities are rising in large parts of the world (see chapter 8). This would seem to lead towards a grim future in which pushing against the digital divide will be an uphill struggle. As the chances for solving both social and digital inequality are very small, we have to conclude that the digital divide cannot be closed but only mitigated. This is the vision behind the solutions proposed in this chapter, which are intended to reduce social and digital inequality *simultaneously*.

The second challenge is to deal with both *absolute and relative inequality* in this context. Absolute inequality is when people are excluded from using digital media. Relative inequality is when some people are benefiting more than others through the use of digital media. The question is whether 'the rich' are getting richer or more powerful by using and benefiting from digital media while 'the poor' are increasingly left behind. Solutions to both absolute and relative inequality will be discussed.

This chapter addresses the problem of the digital divide from the perspectives of both scholars and policy-makers. The first observation to be made here is that the discourses of these two constituencies are quite different and separate. Policy documents virtually ignore the numerous scientific publications mentioned in this book and refer primarily to other policy documents and official statistics. However, it is true that policy research has followed the same focus during the last ten years – the shift of attention from physical access problems to problems of digital skills and usage. Simultaneously, digital divide scholars rarely refer to the work of policy-makers, as policy perspectives are not their prime objective.

The causes of this separation are twofold. First, scholars describe the divide problem mainly with their own data and are only just beginning to formulate a theory explaining the phenomenon (see chapter 2). Thus they are not yet in a position to offer concrete policy directions. Most of their proposals are of a very general kind, such as the suggestions that more attention should be paid to digital skills or that more meaningful applications are the solution to non-use. Second, scholars and policy-makers use different frameworks when dealing with the problem. While the former use general frameworks of empirical description and theoretical explanation, the latter work with the specific frameworks in which they are interested. These interests might be lack of economic growth or innovativeness, labour market deficiencies, or educational policies. There are only a few general government departments or national task groups in particular countries that are dealing with the whole picture of the digital divide problem (see below). While scholars prefer an empirical approach, policy-makers and researchers clearly use a normative approach following the current strategies of government, business and NGOs.

The scientific disciplines of digital divide scholars were described in chapter 2. But who are the policy-makers and researchers? First, there are *national and local governments*, whose departments contain policy researchers and advisors. Second, there are *international bodies*, such as the UN, UNESCO and the European Union, sector institutions such as the ITU (telecommunication), the OECD (economy) and the World Bank (finance), and informal forums such as the World Economic Forum. Allied to these forums are *think tanks or policy journals* such as *The Economist*. Third, there are *national and international NGOs* and *pressure groups* promoting particular goals and issues: social, cultural and public norms and directions, consumer interests, and educational innovation or public awareness about digital media problems.

Fourth, there are stakeholders in the digital media sector itself, the *IT and Telecom companies* which focus on the technical issues of access and connectivity for all and new directions in technical infrastructure, hardware, software and providers. Related to these are the *business producers in the ICT or digital media sector*, responsible for the product design of digital technology. Finally we have *the users themselves*, both businesses as users of ICTs and the individual workers, consumers and citizens with their representatives in trade unions and consumer or citizens' organizations. They also have a responsibility to solve the digital divide by developing awareness about the positive and negative outcomes of digital media use and by organizing or following courses and training to improve their skills. Organizational users and their representatives have their own staff of policy researchers.

In this final chapter I will first discuss the different *goals* of the policies to bridge the digital divide, analysed in five perspectives, following which I will deal with *the means* to realize these perspectives. A number of concrete solutions will be classified according to our four phases of technology appropriation: motivation/attitude, physical access, digital skills and usage. I will then propose my own list of strategic undertakings to fight both digital and social inequality.

Goals: policy perspectives for the digital divide

There are five main policy perspectives to solve or mitigate the digital divide problem related to the different frameworks discussed in chapter 1. I will argue that all these perspectives are necessary and valid; the digital divide problem is much too complicated to be approached with a single or limited strategy. A comparison scheme for the five perspectives is summarized in table 9.1.

The technological perspective

The first international perspective to deal with the digital divide problem is technological, which has the goal of *distributing digital technology* in society.

Table 9.1. Policy perspectives to solve the digital divide and the characteristics of their goals

Perspective	Goal	Primary indices	Focus in phase of appropriation
Technological	Creation and distribution of digital technology	Availability	Physical access
Economic	Support markets, competition and innovation	Affordability	Physical access Usage: collective
Educational	Formal and adult education of ICTs	Readiness	Digital skills
Social	Inclusion and participation of all	Affordability, readiness, relevance	Usage: individual
Persuasive	Awareness	Relevance	Motivation/attitude

This means supporting infrastructure, primarily computer networks but also devices linked by these networks, in order to connect the unconnected. Two decades ago the unconnected were a majority in both developed and developing countries, though today they are a minority in the developed countries.

This perspective dominated during the first level of digital divide research, when the focus was physical access, as described in chapter 4. It is no surprise that physical access should have been the most popular goal at a time when a promising new technology had arrived. The thinking was that everybody should have the opportunities and benefits of this technology. The technological perspective is created, promoted and fed mainly by data from (inter)national IT and telecom companies, technological research institutes and the R&D departments of business and government departments. The most important of these is the International Telecommunication Union (ITU), which continually provides data about the state of connections and the stock of devices available.

General technology diffusion has the goal of *universal access* to the Internet with a particular access device or terminal, in the same way that the telephone and broadcasting became ubiquitous. Focused technology diffusion, on the other hand, connects particular parts of the population who have the greatest access problems. Two possibilities here are *providing public access* (e.g. in libraries and community technology centres) and *distributing* computers and tablets primarily in schools (examples are One Laptop per Child projects and so-called iPad schools). The technology in question is continually changing with the targets of universal and public access. Having begun with PCs and dial-up Internet connections in the 1990s, it shifted to mobile telephones and laptop computers after the year 2000, and since 2010 it has focused on broadband connections (fixed and mobile). Objectives and standards of mobile connections are continually being upgraded, from 2G via 3G and 4G to 5G.

Obviously, creating and distributing digital technology and supporting physical access are necessary goals to bridge the digital divide. However, many others are needed to solve this problem. Moreover, the phase of physical access never ends, partly because of continual technology change, but also on account of wider conceptions of access: material or conditional access and a different quality of technology (see chapter 4; Hilbert 2011a; van Deursen and van Dijk 2019). According to these wider conceptions, the physical access divide is here to stay, even in the rich and technologically advanced countries.

Two critical observations are made in the literature. The first is the technological determinism behind most arguments about this perspective.

Creating and distributing digital technology might *increase* rather than decrease social and digital inequality, both inside and between countries (Fuchs 2009; Pick and Sarkar 2015; Skaletsky et al. 2017; see also the analysis in this book). The second is that the published linear trend projections showing upward curves are unfounded (James 2008). As this and other books have shown, there are too many factors at work to make exact predictions about the future of access.

The economic perspective

The economic perspective often accompanies the technical perspective in the policies of government and business. It assumes that the problem will be solved through a better supply of digital technology, and so the main goal is to *boost investment* in the ICT sector, thus advancing growth and development and enhancing innovation. An assumed side effect is to lower the prices of hardware, software and services. This can be supported by policies to *enhance competition* in the sector.

This perspective is promoted mainly by government departments, international economic and financial institutions such as the OECD, the World Trade Organization and the World Bank, and forums or think thanks such as the World Economic Forum (WEF) and the Economist Intelligence Unit. These organizations are used to making indexes and lists of countries showing their performance and development in access to digital technology. Examples are the annual *Inclusive Internet Index* published by *The Economist* and the *Inclusive Development Index* of the WEF. While these indices are rather superficial and arbitrary, they do use appropriate labels, such as availability, affordability, readiness and relevance.

The main ways in this perspective of bridging the digital divide are more *investment* in digital technology, stimulating *innovation*, and supporting *competition* in the ICT sector. Historically, the choice for investment has always been whether it should be undertaken by the public or the private sector. After the public telecommunication and broadcasting monopolies were dismantled in the 1980s, private firms took over in almost every country. This does not mean that governments no longer invest. In fact the Internet was first set up by the US Defense Department. Today, East Asian governments remain among the main investors in ICT infrastructure.

Innovation is led by small start-up companies and large R&D departments in corporations. Governments stimulate innovation by funding academic research. Competition policy was first enacted to oppose the retreating public monopolies; currently it has to deal with the growing power of the new monopolies on the Internet such as the Big Five American Internet companies. Next to innovation, competition has succeeded in reducing the prices of hardware, software and services. In this way it supported the collective usage of digital media by businesses and consumers and contributed towards closing the digital divide of physical access.

Nevertheless, many assumptions behind the economic perspective are questionable, principal among which is whether ICTs actually boost economic growth (see below; Gordon 2016). Another assumption is that supporting business, innovation and competition in digital technology not only enhances economic growth and development in a country as a whole but also reduces digital divides both inside and between countries. However, almost all research shows that the rate of ICT access and the development of a country is closely related to its GDP and its urbanization (examples are Fuchs 2009; Cruz-Jesus et al. 2018). These indicators are not easy to change through policy.

Research also shows that (un)equal access is related to a great extent to the so-called Gini coefficient of (in)equality and the general level of education (Fuchs 2009; Bauer 2018; Cruz-Jesus et al. 2018). Supporting digital technology through investment, innovation and competition might reduce *absolute* inequality once every country and all its inhabitants have some kind of access. However, it might lead simultaneously to more *relative* inequality between and inside countries (see references just mentioned).

This is a case of uneven and combined development observed in development theory (Hilferding 1981; Milanovic 2016). Combined development in this context is the global accessibility and affordability of digital media. Uneven development is a trend of persistent differences in levels and rates of economic development between various sectors of the economy. The most advanced countries are progressing faster with digital technology than the disadvantaged countries, which, though they may be in a better position than previously, are lagging further and further behind – another case of relative inequality.

The educational perspective

The preceding two perspectives are supply-side policies, while the following perspectives are demand-side led, focusing on users. During the years of second- and third-level digital divide research, the importance of digital literacy and skills for real access was highlighted. The assumption was that, without such skills, people would be unable to take advantage of digital media. Since about 2010 digital literacy and skills have also figured in policy documents.

Supporters of the educational perspective naturally expect the digital divide to be bridged through education and training in both *formal and adult education*. There are four ways of achieving this. The first is to integrate digital literacy or skills into formal education at all levels – not only of students but also of teachers, who often need remedial training. The second is to promote adult education in libraries, community centres and other public places, aimed specifically at people over the age of forty who have not learned digital skills at school. The third is training on the job, and the fourth is stimulating Internet users to learn skills on their own.

While this perspective is emphasized primarily by educational authorities and institutions, community service workers, and social or educational scientists, in the last ten years it also figures increasingly in the general national strategies of government departments and taskforces.

As I have argued in this book, the phase of acquiring digital skills is the most crucial in the process of technology appropriation. However, there are a number of basic problems that the educational perspective cannot solve. First, all unequal resources and structural inequalities will remain (Mariën and Prodnik 2014; Davies and Eynon 2018). At best, their levels can be mitigated by improving digital skills. Second, there has been a stagnation and even a decrease in social mobility in the labour market, the educational system and society at large in many countries of the world, as has been observed in many recent scientific studies and reports of international policy forums such as the OECD, the WEF and the World Bank, which fear the rise of populism. Labour markets are polarizing; educational systems are divided by levels and quality of schooling; and societies are segmented in many domains (see chapter 8). The popular objective of equal opportunities or chances for all is the ideal of *meritocracy*: 'whatever your social position at birth, society ought to offer enough opportunity and mobility for "talent" to combine with "effort" in order to "rise to the top"' (Littler 2018: 1). However, meritocracy is in crisis; the ideal is becoming a liberal or conservative ideology in contrast to social, economic and educational reality (McNamee and Miller 2009; Littler 2018).

After the Second World War in the developed countries, a whole generation of children were able to overtake their parents in social mobility. It is questionable whether the next generation will enjoy the same achievement; it is more likely that things will go in the opposite direction. The rungs of the ladder of mobility are broken (McNamee and Miller 2009; Economist Intelligence Unit 2019; Hayes 2016; Vuyk 2017; Littler 2018). So the question remains whether improving (different) digital skills will support jobs and schools at the bottom or at the top of the ladder.

The social perspective

The core concept of the social perspective is *inclusion*. It is understood as a human right that everyone should be able to participate in the information and network society. Universal access to digital technology is the main goal, and particular attention should be paid to the most deprived groups: seniors, children and adolescents, women, (ethnic) minorities, disabled people and the so-called poor. While inclusion is the assumed result of the first three perspectives, the social perspective (presuming that the technological, economic and educational perspectives will not extend to all groups) focuses on participation in society itself.

In order to bridge the digital divide, the social perspective suggests, first, that the government should provide full access to social and public services and tools of engagement for every citizen, both online and offline. These services will need to be accessed by traditional means for some time yet. Government and other public organizations need to follow the web guidelines for disabled Internet users. Second, concerted action needs to be taken in communities, public places, schools and homes where one finds the most deprived groups. It could be organized by civil servants, social and community workers or public librarians in cooperation with representatives of the deprived groups concerned. This requires special strategies and tactics based on a knowledge of the needs of each particular group. To reach the goals of this perspective, *affordability* is to be supported by (more or less) free provision of basic equipment and software, *readiness* organized via customized courses, for instance in public libraries or community centres, and *relevance* accomplished by creating appropriate content and apps for groups.

This perspective is advocated by social and political scientists, civil servants, community, social and cultural workers, and members of charity organizations. Indeed, charities are often the ones who coordinate arrangements in the field. Social and political scientists investigate opportunities for participation in several domains (Mossberger et al. 2014; Helsper 2012). The social perspective tends to focus on the technology and its opportunities or uses and not on social, economic, political and cultural conditions (Mariën and Prodnik 2014), which are often so serious and permanent that the result of any participatory action is bound to be marginal. But it is difficult to solve the basic problems of deprived groups with technology when in fact the solutions are social.

The persuasive perspective

The last perspective to be discussed here focuses on motivation and attitudes. I have emphasized in this book that these are driving every phase of appropriation. Most reasons given by non-users of digital media are motivational – 'I do not want it' or 'I do not need it' – while others are attitudinal – 'I reject the medium' for its assumed bad features (cybercrime, excessive use and poor communication) (see table 3.1, p. 36). In other words, such individuals are anticipating the negative outcomes of digital media use.

In order to bridge the digital divide, the persuasive perspective concentrates on showing the *relevance* of digital media applications and on creating *awareness* about both positive and negative outcomes. The first way of doing this is to show the usefulness of digital media and the relevance of the content offered, which often means encouraging customized applications and local content for non-users and infrequent users. The second way is to provide information in order to change attitudes. The goal is to create awareness about and trust in positive outcomes of digital media use as well as providing information about how to deal with security and privacy problems and to prevent the excessive and abusive use of digital media. The target groups for such interventions are people with few digital skills and children or young people exhibiting insecure online behaviour.

This perspective is often advocated by scholars of development theory or of social and cultural science. It is practised by NGOs and government departments dealing with social, cultural and development affairs. There are also pressure groups advocating more care in solving security and privacy problems. However, these actors also appeal to those who produce hardware and software and offer services to provide safer, privacy-friendly and useable products for all. Finally, awareness campaigns emphasize the responsibility of users to change their online behaviour.

A major criticism of the persuasive perspective is that it is trying to remedy the characteristics of a technology that is evolving in the wrong direction. Prevention is better than cure: what is needed are designs, products and rules or regulations for useable, secure, privacy-friendly and non-addictive digital media. In awareness campaigns it is mainly the end users who are (morally) addressed rather than the producers, and the social, economic and cultural contexts causing a particular behaviour are not confronted. Most scholars and policy-makers know that mass campaigns usually have small effect on individual behaviour unless the environment concerned is changed at the same time.

The five perspectives discussed are moving forward. At the start of the digital divide problem around the millennium, only the first two perspectives were promulgated, and in fact they remain dominant. However, now even economists, telecom technicians and IT producers make reference in their research and policy documents to the skills, literacy, product relevance and readiness needed to achieve access for all.

International comparison of digital divide policies

The technological and economic perspectives are dominant in all countries, but in recent years there has been a shift towards the social and persuasive perspectives. Global policies are offered by several UN institutions, the ITU, the OECD, the World Bank and the World Economic Forum. National policies can be proposed by separate government departments or taskforces combining departments, by national commissions or by institutions supporting employment and innovation.

Hilbert does not believe in national strategies: he argues that their investments and achievements are unknown and suggests another approach: 'it is not the existence or non-existence of a national strategy per se that explains success of failure in digital development, but rather sector-specific projects and tailor-made policies that address specific areas of interest' (Hilbert 2011b: 731). Such projects and policies can best be undertaken at a regional and local level with a multi-stakeholder strategy (World Bank 2016). However, national strategies do reflect the various approaches in the world to the digital divide. I will now give a very brief summary of these strategies in the main regions of the developed countries and the economically emerging and developing countries. For more detailed descriptions, see Peña-López (2009), Hilbert (2011b) and World Bank (2016).

North America

The concept of the digital divide arose in the United States and was already part of the Clinton–Gore government agenda in the 1990s. Since that time, the Federal Communications Commission (FCC) and the National Telecommunications and Information Administration (NTIA) have undertaken research, given policy advice and developed regulations. They also inspired or organized annual budgets of billions of dollars for national programmes, though by far the most investment came from federal departments and agencies (Hilbert 2011b). For the last twenty years there have been federal programmes such as the Universal Service Fund connecting schools, libraries and community technology and technology opportunities programmes serving local innovation projects. Similar programmes have been available at the state level.

After the installation of the Bush administration in 2001, the budgets of all these technology diffusion programmes were severely reduced. At that time the assumption was that the digital divide was beginning to close and that the market would solve the problem completely. In 2009 the Obama administration set up the Broadband Technology Opportunities Program (NTIA 2009), which focused on a nationwide deployment of broadband access. The most important digital divide in the US today is the growing gap between broadband and narrow access and between people using PCs and laptops at home and those who have only smartphones with limited data (Mossberger et al. 2012, 2014; Skaletsky et al. 2017; Levine and Taylor 2018). Current American policy to bridge the digital divide is to provide public access across the board. Home access is not an official objective.

In diffusion and innovation, the US demonstrates a clear technological perspective (supply orientation) and economic perspective (a market approach of both supply and demand). The social, educational and persuasive perspectives are left to the educational sector, public access provision and local community development. No further public investment in the distribution of computers and staffing (training), except for the educational sector, is considered appropriate. A very specific trait of the American situation is the important role of philanthropists such as Bill and Melinda Gates in donating computers and Internet connections to schools, libraries, computer technology centres and teacher training institutions.

A final characteristic feature of the situation in the US is the small part played by public enterprise in model projects, awareness programmes and special content and application development to stimulate underserved users, minorities, the disabled and the illiterate. Most private initiatives are undertaken by hardware and software producers and public–private associations, sometimes in cooperation with community organizations.

There is much greater government initiative in dealing with the digital divide in Canada, where there is a large urban–rural digital divide, even wider than that in the US (Mallett et al. 2017). The Canadian government strategy in the 1990s was called Connecting Canadians and was very broad; it contained six pillars (Steinour 2001), which were policies not only to extend universal access via infrastructure but also to support local communities in establishing pilot demonstration projects, to increase Canadian content online, to organize the country's school networks, and to promote e-commerce and e-government.

East Asia

East Asia has become one of the most important strongholds of ICT production and diffusion in the world and now surpasses North America and Europe in broadband capacity (Broadband Commission 2018). It specializes in the manufacture of hardware and has become the main exporter of computer equipment and network technology. South Korea has the widest broadband coverage in the world. However, there is a clear divide between more advanced countries in the region (South Korea, Japan, Singapore, Hong Kong and Taiwan) and less developed countries such as Indonesia and the Philippines. The emerging economy of China is catching up rapidly, with astonishing growth figures of more than 50 per cent Internet coverage in 2018.

East Asian countries reveal a strong emphasis on government initiative in order to stimulate the private-sector manufacture of ICT. These states make strategic and selective interventions in the economy to promote and sustain development but leave most of its execution to private enterprise. This is the situation in China, where the government's Five-Year Plans are realized mainly by large companies financed by the Chinese Bank and ministries. Even before 2000, influential ministries in most East Asian countries launched and coordinated nationwide plans to promote digital media in society. Examples in the first decade of the twenty-first century are the Technopolis programme in Japan, the Singapore One Project, the Malaysian Super Corridor Project and the Cyber Korea 21 initiative. The ultimate aim of these plans, which adhered strongly to the technological and economic perspectives, was to accomplish universal service, not by funds and subsidies as in the US or by regulation as in the EU, but by galvanizing the national telecom companies and electronics manufacturers to roll out infrastructure and to produce equipment that will eventually extend to every household.

The assumption was that this diffusion of general technology, accompanied by nationwide awareness campaigns, would lead to wide-scale adoption of the Internet. In a third phase, digital skills and useful applications for the economy and society would be promoted. Unfortunately, this staged approach can lead to stagnation after a time because digital skills, user experience and local development have to be organized in parallel. This warning was expressed early on by critical observers such as Wong (2002) and Shin (2007). After an incredible uptake of broadband access throughout South Korea lasting about twenty years, these observers have been shown to be right. The gap in physical access between parts of the population (social class) have largely disappeared, but the gaps in digital skills and usage remain substantial (Park and Kim 2014).

In the last fifteen years, the national policies of East Asian countries have paid greater attention to the social, educational and persuasive perspectives. South Korea was the first, with the launch of their plan *Bridging the Digital Divide* (KADO 2003). This had more focus on digital skills, usage inequalities and disadvantaged groups than for example the US and Europe had at that time. However, awareness is not the same thing as achievement. The Chinese government also wants to reduce the enormous gap in Internet access and use between the urban and rural population and between the poor and the rich (Ben et al. 2017). In fact, the (relative) gaps in access, skills and usage between city and region and between poor and rich are persistent and even growing (Ben et al. 2017; ITU 2017).

The technological and economic perspectives remain dominant in East Asia, as is testified by the latest plans such as the *Digital Economy Framework for Action* in Singapore (IMDA 2018) and the 13th Five-Year Plan for National Informatization in China (2016–20) (Ben et al. 2017).

Europe

North-Western Europe is ahead in physical access as compared to the United States and most East Asian countries (ITU 2017; Ben et al. 2017; WEF 2018; Broadband Commission 2018). However, the Southern and Eastern European countries are lagging far behind, with access figures at only about half the rate of their neighbours (Digital Economy and Society Index 2018; ITU 2017; Ben et al. 2017; WEF 2018).

The European Union (twenty-eight member states in 2018) is very much engaged with an all-inclusive information society, having produced documents between 1995 and 2010 with titles such as *An Information Society for All*. However, it is the economic perspective, stimulating technological innovation and diffusion, that is dominant in the EU. The main goal is to create a common market and to reduce the gap between North-Western and South-Eastern countries using such plans as *Connectivity for a Competitive Digital Single Market* (European Commission 2016a).

The major strategic route taken by the EU is to liberalize telecommunications and the whole media sector. Building and distributing the new infrastructure is left to the market. It is questionable whether the policy of stimulating innovation and then correcting the market through regulation is successful (see ETNO annual reports 2016 and 2017). European Internet companies have been left standing by American and Chinese companies, and the EU today has more problems regulating the big American Internet platforms than in liberalizing their own media companies.

As the (Western) European countries purport to be welfare states, in theory they should redistribute resources, be they hardware, software, services or training opportunities, to people who have little or no access. However, this has not happened. The EU's information society policy has shifted to a technological and market focus, and the European Structural and Investment Funds for innovation and R&D have to be directed towards new business opportunities. Public national and local government investment is organized by the member states themselves in the field of education and to support particular problem areas or groups. It focuses on educational resources, public access, community-building, and some assistance to the unemployed, people living on social benefits, and low-income families with school-age children.

Taking all spending into account, it seems that articulated government investment in closing the digital divide is considerably more generous in the EU than in the US, but lower than in East Asia (see the balance of European public investment in Rubio et al. 2016). However, it is impossible to measure the precise overall public investment in ICTs in all these countries.

One of the most important differences in digital divide policy between the EU, the US and East Asia is the much bigger role in Europe for public awareness-building programmes and the promotion of the information society (Servaes and Burgelman 2000). A major proportion of EU funding goes to model and awareness projects. Besides, more regulation is proposed to transform the Internet into a safer environment for users. In this way Europe pays comparatively more attention to a persuasive perspective. More recently, there has also been an educational perspective with the publication of *A New Skills Agenda for Europe* (European Commission 2016b; see also Helsper and van Deursen 2015; Cruz-Jesus et al. 2016). The European Commission has discovered that a lack of digital skills in the workplace has caused a fall in productivity and in consumption in the digital market. A majority of European employers take no action to improve the digital skills of their employees (Ecorys and DTI 2016).

The developing world

In the developing countries, by 2017 Internet access was reached by an average of 40 per cent of the population, though in the least developed countries (LDCs) the figure was less than 20 per cent (ITU 2017). This was achieved mainly by an amazing upsurge in mobile telephony: 80 per cent of people in developing countries have a mobile phone, about half of whom have a mobile Internet connection. However, most people use a *feature phone* with very few Internet options; only a minority own a smartphone (3G), and fewer still have a 4G mobile phone that can actually be called broadband (ITU 2017).

The spectacular success of mobile telephony in the developing world inspired policy-makers and scholars with the idea that these countries could 'leapfrog' the construction of an expensive fixed infrastructure of cable, copper and fibre lines realized in the developed world and immediately transfer to a mobile network (James 2003). This idea is contested (see below), but the most important conclusion is that it testifies to a techno-logical solution to bridging the digital divide. A second perspective makes the assumption that deploying ICT infrastructure enhances the economic, social and cultural development of developing countries as a whole. This too is challenged. The counter-arguments are 1) that deploying infrastructure is not a cause but an effect of economic development and 2) that such effects lead to combined and unequal development: the rich and most parts of the developing countries can be linked to the world market and advanced tech-nology, while the poor, most often rural parts of these countries are lagging behind more and more. The rural and urban divide is the most important problem both in emerging economies such as China and in the LDCs.

These doubts raise the basic question as to which *strategy of development* bridging the digital divide is best for the developing countries (Mutsvairo and Ragnedda 2019). Four strategies are available (van Dijk 2005). The first is to adopt some kind of staged approach, such as the one conducted in East Asia, first rolling out the technical infrastructure such as mobile broadband and promoting a local industry of ICT production and/or software develop-ment. The second stage is to invest in medium-related digital skills, first for those who need it most, then for the whole population, and the final stage is to develop usage applications for everybody and teach content-related skills in schools.

A second strategy is a strong version of a staged approach: leapfrog the development phases and go directly to the deployment of infrastructure and the manufacture and servicing of ICT in industrial regions directly linked to the world market. This is what India and some East Asian countries have done.

The third strategy is the opposite of the staged approach. It is argued that Third World countries can evolve only gradually from their present state. A large-scale distribution of information and communication technology is not at present the most important goal. In its place, all energy should be devoted to basic material and human resources – working electricity, transport, health, basic education and media such as the press, broadcasting and telephony. Surprisingly, this strategy was also suggested in a speech by the founder of Microsoft, Bill Gates: 'I am suggesting that if somebody is interested in equity that you wouldn't spend more than twenty per cent of your time talking about access to computers, that you'd get back to literacy and health and things like that. So the balance that makes sense is that more money should be spent on malaria' (Gates 2000).

The final strategy is a rejection of all stage approaches and proposes that investment in technical infrastructure, education and usage applications should be made in parallel (Mansell and When 1998). Clearly, this strategy fits best with the core argument of this book. However, the four successive phases of technology appropriation by *individuals* are not stages of diffusion in the development of *countries*. The only conclusion derived from the theory and model of phases of technology appropriation is that technical, social, economic, cultural and educational resources have to be deployed equally for development to take place.

All five policy perspectives discussed here are needed to mitigate the digital divides in developing countries. From the *technological perspective*, the most popular strategy is to go mobile. Indeed, the explosive growth of mobile telephony and the Internet has provided a taste of the opportunities inherent in media networking for the peoples of Africa, Asia and South America: better communication, services and basic information for everyday life. Messaging is cheaper than calling. Health information is in close reach and hospitals can be contacted. Government and other public services are available online. The latest information about food prices and diseases, agricultural technique and irrigation can be retrieved. All of this is very important to boost the motivation for and relevance of digital media use.

However, the developing countries cannot 'leapfrog' the diffusion of digital technology simply by going mobile and would in fact remain stuck in their current stage of development. Mobile phones are powerful tools for *existing* production, circulation, consumption and communication; they support current agriculture, trade and the formal economy in these countries, but they do not create a new mode of production to compete in the world market. To reach a higher stage of development, what is needed is the construction of a fixed infrastructure of huge computer centres and fibre or copper cable networks, with mobile only at the so-called local loop for reaching users, all of which requires enormous investment. China has understood this and is currently preparing the relevant infrastructure (Shenglin et al. 2017). In the meantime, what is called for is general broadband access in public buildings, community centres and Internet cafés.

From the economic perspective, ICTs offer a good means of entry for small and medium-sized business start-ups in mobile phone rental and repair, computer training and data entry or software, telephony services for international companies, and Internet cafés. A reasonable level of access to the Internet and the global information infrastructure is required to be able to participate in the trend of outsourcing of production from the high-tech economies to the newly industrializing economies.

The most important conditions necessary to achieve this are a working infrastructure (reliable electricity and connections), educational resources (literacy, school attendance, participation of girls) and political institutions (regulation and a working system of law to fight corruption). Without these conditions the digital divide will certainly not be mitigated.

From the educational perspective, just providing schools with computers and Internet connections is not enough (see the criticism of the One Laptop per Child strategy below). More basic investment has to be made, such as building more schools, training teachers (not only in digital skills), enabling children – especially girls – to go to (a higher level of) school, developing better curricula and providing the old medium of textbooks.

From the social perspective, public access is crucial. Next to adequate mobile connections, the availability of public access points with broadband capacity is needed to reach at least a basic measure of social inclusion.

Perhaps the best strategy is offered by the persuasive perspective. We have seen what a boost to mobile connections and opportunities has achieved. Showing the relevance of digital media for people in the developing world is the best incentive (Mwim and Kritzinger 2016), which means producing applications and content in the national or regional language which fit their needs (see some examples provided above). The worst strategy is to impose provisions, programmes, approaches and content from the developed, most often Western, countries.

Means: solutions to bridge the digital divide

All five perspectives are required in order to find the specific solutions to bridge or mitigate the digital divide. This section will propose about twenty solutions for solving the digital divide problem organized along the four phases of general access. In an earlier book (van Dijk 2005) I portrayed them as the spokes of a wheel; figure 9.1 is an updated version, though, surprisingly, not much has changed during the last fifteen years.

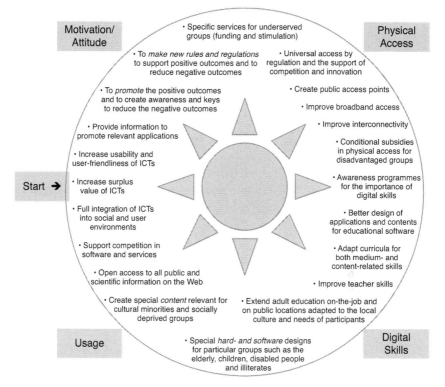

Figure 9.1. A wheel of policy instruments to bridge the digital divide

Motivation and attitude

The primary drivers of motivation and attitude are temporal and material resources (chapter 3). Thus having children in school or adults in a job where they have to use computers and the Internet is the best solution to create positive motivations and attitudes. Mental resources driven by a particular intelligence, literacy, technical ability and personality are also relevant, but these cannot always be changed.

Another influence comes from social and cultural resources. In a context where large numbers of people are using digital media and offering support, others will be motivated too. Social and communication needs are the initial way of bringing people to the Internet, as is shown today by the very fast adoption of mobile telephony and social media in the developing countries. Cultural resources – in particular the content manifested on the Internet and other digital media – are the last important driver of digital media use.

So, a first solution to bridge the digital divide where motivation is concerned is *to increase the surplus value of digital media* as compared to traditional media. This means creating relevant applications and attractive content for every group of users. In the 1980s and 1990s, the Internet clearly belonged to young, highly educated, male, rich, able-bodied Western users speaking English. Today, while many other people are using the Internet, there still are many minorities – cultural, ethnic, social and personal (people with various handicaps) – who could be offered more motivation. Examples are providing apps for migrants in their own language, web access and assistance for the homeless, housing and job-finding apps focused on the poor or on people with insecure jobs, and aids for disabled people for easier access to and use of the web.

The second solution evidently is *increasing the usability and user-friendliness* of digital media for all – a task for the companies and the organizations offering websites, software and other apps aimed at the general public. Both usability and the user-friendliness of digital media have dramatically improved in the last thirty years, but they remain a challenge because applications have become ever more complicated and because there are increasing numbers of users with low abilities.

A third solution is to *provide information to promote relevant applications*. This might involve public campaigns for healthy living, education, finding a job or community participation. However, it might also mean creating more awareness about the positive outcomes of Internet use. Recent research shows that most people have only a general idea about the positive (and negative) outcomes of Internet use (chapter 7). If they became more conscious of the specific benefits of e-commerce, e-government and e-health or finding jobs and educational opportunities online, they might be more motivated to use the Internet.

This brings us to the attitudes which inspire people to want to use digital media. The first solution to bridge the digital divide is to *promote the positive outcomes and to create awareness of and ways of reducing the negative outcomes* of digital media use. This may be a task for government, educational and NGO actors, who need to show clear positive outcomes in the domains of the labour market, education, health and community. They might also show ways of preventing or mitigating negative outcomes of excessive use, abuse and the lack of secure and privacy-friendly online behaviour. The main goal here is to support *trust* in digital media.

Promotion and creation of awareness will have no effect if governments and public institutions make no *new rules and regulations to promote positive outcomes and to prevent negative outcomes*, particularly in the domains of economic competition, security and privacy. The most urgent task today is to regulate the social media platforms and their use, since these present the greatest problems in terms of monopolization, cyber abuse, disinformation, manipulation and loss of privacy.

Physical access

According to chapter 4, lack of material resources is the cause of the huge gap in physical access between the developed and developing countries, as well as inside many countries. This situation continues because income inequality is rising in most parts of the world (chapter 8), and neither governments nor employers are able or willing to take action to improve matters. Other causes, such as social and cultural resources, arise from people's choices. However, governments have the duty to organize universal and public access. *Universal access* can be defined as 'access to a defined minimum service of specified quality to all users independent of their geographical locations and, in the light of specific national conditions, at an affordable price' (European Commission 1996). *Public access* is the provision of information and communication connections, information sources and places where hardware, software and connections required are freely available, for instance in libraries, community centres, municipal halls and schools, and perhaps free public wifi for people to use their own devices. Public access is a substitute where a country cannot afford universal access, which is often the case in developing countries.

Organizing physical access for all requires enormous investment, which is one of the reasons why, in the last thirty years, most governments have left this task to private companies. Only in East Asia is there a sizeable amount of public or government investment (see below). Elsewhere, governments tend to subsidize R&D and academic research and try to realize *universal access by regulation* and *through market competition*. For instance, private suppliers are required to connect not only urban areas, with several subscribers, but also remote, more sparsely populated regions at the same price; this applies equally to broadband connections. Public regulatory institutions also stimulate a *better interconnectivity* between different channels or carriers such as the original telephone, satellite and cable television channels. Governments do still invest in *public access*, particularly in the developing countries, where at least mobile access to the Internet is required.

Today, *broadband access* is the main priority in both developed and developing countries. In the US this is the only remaining governmental infrastructure policy. In developing countries broadband access for all is needed to prevent a situation where the majority have only 2G connections and only members of the elite have 3G smartphones (Schoemaker 2014; Reed et al. 2014; Skaletsky et al. 2017; Broadband Commission 2018). The difference between narrow- and broadband connections is the most important divide in physical access today (Napoli and Obar 2014; Schoemaker 2014; Reed et al. 2014; Levine and Taylor 2018).

A highly contested subject of debate is whether governments should directly *subsidize physical access for disadvantaged groups*. According to my analysis, undirected provision of computers or connections is not an effective strategy (van Dijk 2005), though strictly *conditional* subsidies in particular situations might make sense. Target groups might be the long-term unemployed, the homeless, people below the poverty line, migrants trying to find a job, and disabled people needing aids or peripherals to use computers, with individuals required to take certain courses and use job-search or job-training sites.

Digital skills

Provided that sufficient temporal and material resources are available, mental resources are the most important causes of divides in obtaining digital skills (see chapter 5). In this context, intelligence aside, mental resources are technical proficiency or know-how, knowledge of technological and societal affairs, and analytic capabilities all of which can be developed through social contacts and education.

However, education is actually the final step in solving the problem of a lack of skills. In *Digital Skills*, van Dijk and van Deursen (2014) dedicated a full chapter to digital skills policies, starting with awareness and improving the design of digital technology and moving on to the provision of technology, such as connecting schools and providing public access. Also important is content development: educational software, curriculum change and certification of modules in skills programmes. Only then does the teaching of digital skills in formal and adult education take place.

Organizing *awareness programmes* as to the importance of digital skills can be done by labour, educational and government representatives. This issue is not given priority in many labour organizations and even in schools. Individuals often overestimate their own skills (see chapter 5), which means that *institutional and self-assessments* have to be undertaken and monitored.

Learning digital skills is much easier if there is a *good design of applications and content*. Another aspect is to adapt hardware and software for particular groups: seniors, the illiterate, disabled people, especially the visually impaired, and those of very low intelligence. Examples are extra aids for reading screens and following the accessibility standards for websites.

Many policy-makers believe that connecting and equipping schools and public access points with computers and the Internet is also the starting point for learning digital skills. In poor countries and regions this is indeed a necessity. However, several social and educational scientists are critical about One Laptop per Child projects and establishing so-called iPad schools (Warschauer and Ames 2010; Selwyn 2013; van Dijk and van Deursen 2014). Simply providing hardware and software without sufficient guidance and educational innovation and without taking into account the local culture is bound to fail. Instead of an approach of 'simply handing computers to children and walking away, there needs to be large-scale integrated educational improvement.' The poor countries 'would be better off building schools, training teachers, developing curricula, providing books and subsidizing attendance' (Warschauer and Ames 2010: 34).

Content development links more directly to the practice of learning digital skills. First of all the meaning of digital skills, including twenty-first-century skills, has to be established (see van Dijk and van Deursen 2014; van Laar et al. 2017). Currently, only very general frameworks are offered (see chapter 5); concrete standardization and certifications are only available for the more technical medium-related skills, such as those of ICDL (International Computer Driving Licence) training centres. Content-related skills standards and twenty-first-century skills definitions are still in the making. One of the latest challenges is learning to cope with the growing disinformation and manipulation on the web. There are no generally accepted educational programmes available in schools and adult education to deal with this problem.

Another task is to create more and better *educational software* appropriate not only for average learners but also for particular target groups (juniors, seniors, cultural minorities, illiterates and teachers themselves).

Finally, it is necessary to support formal education at all levels, adult education, both online and in specific institutions, and on-the-job training or special ICT courses. For formal education, appropriate *curriculum change* has to be made. The best option is not to create special classes but substantially to integrate digital and twenty-first-century skills into every school subject. Policy-makers could also benefit from people's personal experience: for the young, the digital world they know best is quite different from the world of books and chalkboards at school. These experiences should be integrated in all regular computer or Internet courses (see suggestions in Davies and Eynon 2018).

Many teachers in the developed countries have not learned digital skills themselves in school, and so they expect that their young students will have better medium-related skills. However, these young people do not have the necessary content-related skills, so *teacher training* is required to facilitate this (van Dijk and van Deursen 2014).

Learning digital skills has to be integrated into daily life, and in workplaces this means *on-the-job training*. In some countries, such as Canada and Scotland, conditional *funds for every citizen after school life* are considered. Today, government should invest not only in formal education but also in lifelong learning by adults. Courses in libraries, community centres, hospitals and other public buildings should be *adapted to the local culture and the specific needs* of participants.

Usage

In chapter 6 it was found that divides in digital media use arose from social and cultural resources as well as material resources (income) and temporal resources (time). Having a particular job, attending a particular school, enjoying a relationship network and belonging to a particular family influence the frequency and type of use.

These conclusions show that potential solutions should always be relevant and adapted to the particular needs, social relationships, lifestyles and cultures of potential users. At workplaces they should support *learning on the job* and in homes they should *fit the chosen lifestyle*. The first solution is *special hardware and software* designed for particular groups such as the elderly, children (with special attention to girls), the disabled and those who are functionally illiterate. A second solution is to *create special content relevant for cultural minorities and socially deprived groups*, which most often means local content adapted to the needs of these groups in their own language. This is the main way of providing relevance, a goal that is becoming a part of current policy documents, even those of technical and economic policy-makers.

A third solution, also focused on relevant content, is to *stimulate open access to all public and scientific information* on the Internet. This means not only free government, community and health information or public broadcasting and news media but also greater provision of freeware and shareware for applications that are currently unaffordable for people on low incomes. This also means *supporting competition in software and services* and breaking up old (public) monopolies and new (platform) monopolies. There has to be a way of preventing people with low incomes and education from having to obtain news from cheap and unreliable sources such as Facebook while quality newspapers online remain available only to those with high income and education.

The last solution is the most important general strategy advocated here. This is the *full integration of digital media into social user environments*. So far, digital divide policy, from creating physical access through to digital skills training, has had a mainly technical orientation. Digital technology was presented as something different. Providing the necessary hardware, developing digital skills and installing digital projects in local communities were alien strategies. To be effective, the local needs, languages and existing approaches towards daily activities have to be integrated in every digital strategy. Only this will motivate potential users (see figure 9.1).

These policy instruments to reduce the digital divide are quite general. More specific solutions can be found in national policy documents adapted to local needs. One of the best and complete documents of this nature is *Digital New Zealanders* (Digital Inclusion Research Group 2017), which makes use of the same phases of access as this book (motivation, physical access, skills and usage). It was inspired by a similar document, the *UK Digital Strategy 2017* (www.gov.uk/government/publications/uk-digital-strategy/uk-digital-strategy).

Leverage in the fight against both social and digital inequality

In order to find solutions that not only mitigate the digital divide but also touch both digital and social inequality systematically, I propose the following five undertakings:

- maintain or revitalize social mobility
- increase the number of long-term social programmes adapted to disadvantaged groups in their own communities
- provide cheaper digital technology
- design digital technology that is easier to use
- draw up rules and regulations to manage the beneficial use of digital media.

The first and most important of these is to *maintain or revitalize social mobility*, which we have seen stagnating or decreasing in many countries. In addition to governments establishing income policies, public and private corporations should create jobs and organize rotation schemes and continual learning with special computer courses at all levels. This does not mean arranging a flexible labour market. This flexibility in practice means a hold on any lifelong learning because employers have no interest in schooling employees who are likely to leave in a year or so. Nevertheless, employers have to be stimulated to contribute to lifelong learning, for instance through government direction and support. To reduce the usage gap, employees should be allowed to learn more advanced applications than are needed for their specific jobs. Developed welfare states have to maintain or reinstall safety nets for workers and unemployed people that allow them to find better jobs and undertake lifelong learning, including digital skills (Mounk 2018). In primary and secondary education, digital learning should focus at all levels not only on medium-related skills but also on content-related skills.

The second undertaking is to increase the number of *long-term social programmes for disadvantaged groups in their own communities*. Here social programmes can be integrated with digital skills programmes involving the most relevant applications focusing on housing, job search, health assistance and local culture. This local orientation is also valid for developing countries. See the full integration of digital media into user environments solutions discussed above.

Evidently, providing *cheaper digital technology* will improve physical access for all. Despite today's lower prices, the proliferation of devices, software, subscriptions, services and costs of training consume an increasing proportion of the household budget in both developing and developed countries. The cost of a smartphone in a developing country can equate to several months or even a year of income. Supporting competition in the marketplace is not the only solution here. Hardware, software, content and services should be provided in locations accessible to the public and all vital information should be(come) free on the web.

The next undertaking is *to design digital technology that is easier to use*. Accessible and user-friendly applications provide the most important solution for people with low intelligence, the functionally illiterate and people with particular disabilities. However, while all the new digital applications based on artificial intelligence mean that they are easier to use, the autonomous and automatic decisions made on behalf of the user have to be understood and accepted. This demands the most complex digital skills: strategic skills backed by information skills.

The last undertaking is to draw up *rules and regulations to manage the beneficial use of digital and social media*. In the last ten years, social media platforms have produced serious problems – excessive use, abuse of all kinds, disinformation or manipulation and privacy or security problems – that have caused harm, in particular, to people on the wrong side of the digital divide. These platforms are private companies that evolved into monopolies, and they need to create effective rules for the behaviour of their users. Governments and other public bodies also have the duty to regulate the operation of these platforms, otherwise the difference between knowledgeable, wise, and experienced users, on the one hand, and those who lack the requisite knowledge and experience, on the other, will become one of the most important manifestations of the digital divide.

Future directions

National strategies have done a good job in creating awareness about the coming digital era and problems such as the digital divide. Today, access to digital technology is no longer a great issue. Tailor-made policies addressing specific problems of, for instance, the labour market, innovation, competition, education and community development are now on the agenda. Increasingly, actions to bridge the digital divide will be a task not for (inter) national government and industrial-sector policy institutions but for government, business and educational actors in the field, as well as, ultimately, for users themselves.

We have seen that, in national policies, a shift has occurred from mere technological and economic perspectives to social, educational and persuasive perspectives. However, because digital technology is evolving rapidly and economic growth, productivity and innovation are continuing priorities, the technological and economic perspectives remain dominant.

In the technological domain we see recurring cycles of appropriation when new digital media arrive: the Internet of Things, virtual and augmented reality, and hardware, programs and systems controlled by data and artificial intelligence. Again and again, the first to embrace these developments are the people with high education and income and young people. The digital divide problem seems to be the same but also different with all these media. Increasingly the importance of content-related skills and strategic usage will become the most important issue.

In the economic domain, changes in the economy will be interweaved with changes in digital technology. This also means that the digital divide problem will be less a marginal problem for disadvantaged groups in society than one for the whole workforce, citizenry, the market and its consumers. Robert Gordon (2016) has shown that, so far, the productivity of information and communication technology in America has been disappointing, less than former technologies. We are still waiting for a substantial contribution of digital technology to economic growth. One of the reasons is the digital divide, especially the lack of digital and twenty-first-century skills and omnipresent digital media use that also improves production and not only distribution and consumption.

The final direction of development is the full integration of all digital and social policies. In all domains and perspectives, technical and educational or social approaches have to be combined. This book has shown that social and digital inequality have in fact become the same thing.

References

Ajzen, I. (1991) The theory of planned behavior, *Organizational Behavior and Human Decision Processes*, 50(2): 179–211.

Ajzen, I., and Fishbein, M. (2005) The influence of attitudes on behavior, in D. Albarracin, B. T. Johnson, and M. P. Zanna (eds), *Handbook of Attitudes*, Vol. 1: *Basic Principles*. Mahwah, NJ: Erlbaum, pp. 173–221.

Akiyoshi, M., and Ono, H. (2008) The diffusion of mobile Internet in Japan, *Information Society*, 24(5): 292–303.

Alkali, Y. E., and Amichai-Hamburger, Y. (2004) Experiments in digital literacy, *CyberPsychology & Behavior*, 7(4): 421–9.

Amichai-Hamburger, Y., Fine, A., and Goldstein, A. (2004) The impact of Internet interactivity and need for closure on consumer preference, *Computers in Human Behavior*, 20(1): 103–17.

Anderson, R. H., Bikson, T. K., Law, S. A., and Mitchell, B. M. (eds) (1995) *Universal Access to E-mail: Feasibility and Societal Implications*. Santa Monica, CA: RAND.

Anderson, M., and Perrin, A. (2017) Disabled Americans are less likely to use technology, Pew Research Center Fact Tank, www.pewresearch.org/fact-tank/2017/04/07/disabled-americans-are-less-likely-to-use-technology/.

Anderson, E. L., Steen, E., and Stavropoulos, V. (2017) Internet use and problematic internet use: a systematic review of longitudinal research trends in adolescence and emergent adulthood, *International Journal of Adolescence and Youth*, 22(4): 430–54.

Anderson, J., and Rainie, L. (2018) *Stories from Experts about the Impact of Digital Life*. Washington, DC: Pew Research Center.

Anduiza, E., Jensen, M. J., and Jorba, L. (2012) *Digital Media and Political Engagement Worldwide*. New York: Cambridge University Press.

Anttiroiko, A. V., Lintilä, L., and Savolainen, R. (2001) Information society competencies of managers: conceptual considerations, in E. Pantzar, R. Savolainen, and P. Tynjälä (eds), *In Search for a Human-Centered Information Society*. Tampere: Tampere University Press, pp. 27–57.

Attewell, P. (2001) Comment: the first and second digital divides, *Sociology of Education*, 74(3): 252–9.

Bandura, A. (1991) Social cognitive theory of self-regulation, *Organizational Behavior and Human Decision Processes*, 50(2): 248–87.

Bandura, A. (2001) Social cognitive theory: an agentic perspective, *Annual Review of Psychology*, 52: 1–26.

Bao, P., Pierce, J., Whittaker, S., and Zhai, S. (2011) Smart phone use by non-mobile business users, *Proceedings of the 13th International Conference on Human Computer Interaction with Mobile Devices and Services*, Stockholm, August 30 – September 2, pp. 445–54.

Barberá, P. (2015) *How Social Media Reduces Mass Political Polarization: Evidence from Germany, Spain, and the U.S.*, working paper, http://pablobarbera.com/static/barbera_polarization_APSA.pdf.

Barney, D. (2004) *The Network Society*. Cambridge: Polity.

Bauer, J. M. (2018) The internet and income inequality: socio-economic challenges in a hyperconnected society, *Telecommunications Policy*, 42(4): 333–43.

Bawden, D. (2008) Origins and concepts of digital literacy, in C. Lankshear and M. Knobel (eds), *Digital Literacies: Concepts, Policies and Practices*. New York: Peter Lang, pp. 17–32.

Bawden, D., and Robinson, L. (2001) Training for information literacy: diverse approaches, in *Online Information-international Meeting*. Hampshire UK: Learned Information Ltd, pp. 87–90.

Ben, S., Bosc, R., Jiao, J., Li, W., Simonelli, F., and Zhang, R. (2017) *Digital Infrastructure: Overcoming the Digital Divide in China and the European Union*. Brussels: Centre for European Policy Studies.

Bennett, T., Savage, M., Silva, E., Warde, A., Gayo-Cal, M., and Wright, D. (2009) *Culture, Class, Distinction*. London: Routledge.

Berrío Zapata, C., and Sant'Ana, R. G. (2015) *The Voices of the Digital Divide: A Deconstruction of the Discourse within Information Technology*, working paper presented at WAPOR Buenos Aires, www.waporbuenosaires2015.org/uploads/3/7/6/6/37666309/h4_-_the_voices_of_the_digital_divide_-_berrio-zapata_santana.pdf.

Binkley, M., Erstad, O., Herman, J., Raizen, S., Ripley, M., Miller-Ricci, M., and Rumble, M. (2012) Defining twenty-first century skills, in P. Griffin, B. McGraw and E. Care (eds), *Assessment and Teaching of 21st Century Skills*. Dordrecht: Springer, pp. 17–66.

Blank, G. (2013) Who creates content? Stratification and content creation on the internet, *Information, Communication & Society*, 16(4): 590–612.

Blank, G., and Groselj, D. (2014) Dimensions of internet use: amount, variety, and types, *Information, Communication & Society*, 17(4): 417–35.

Blank, G., and Lutz, C. (2018) Benefits and harms from internet use: a differentiated analysis of Great Britain, *New Media & Society*, 20(2): 618–40.

Boelhouwer, J., Gijsberts, M., and Vrooman, C. (2014) Nederland in meervoud [Netherlands in the plural], in C. Vrooman, M. Gijsberts and J. Boelhouwer (eds), *Verschil in Nederland* [Differences in the Netherlands]. The Hague: Sociaal en Cultureel Planbureau, pp. 283–319.

Bonfadelli, H. (2002) The internet and knowledge gaps: a theoretical and empirical investigation, *European Journal of Communication*, 17(1): 65–84.

Boulianne, S. (2009) Does internet use affect engagement? A meta-analysis of research, *Political Communication*, 26(2): 193–211.

Bourdieu, P. (1986) The forms of capital, in I. Szeman and T. Kaposy (eds), *Cultural Theory: An Anthology*. Chichester: Wiley-Blackwell, pp. 81–93.

Bourdieu, P. (1987) What makes a social class? On the theoretical and practical existence of groups, *Berkeley Journal of Sociology*, 32: 1–17.

Bourdieu, P. ([1979] 2010) *Distinction: A Social Critique of the Judgement of Taste*. New York: Routledge.

Bourdieu, P., and Passeron, J.-C. (1990) *Reproduction in Education, Society and Culture*. 2nd edn, Thousand Oaks, CA: Sage.

Brady, M. (2000) The digital divide myth, *E-commerce Times*, August 4.

Brandtzæg, P. B. (2010) Towards a unified media-user typology (MUT): a meta-analysis and review of the research literature on media-user typologies, *Computers in Human Behavior*, 26(5): 940–56.

Broadband Commission for Sustainable Development (2018) *The State of Broadband 2018: Broadband Catalyzing Sustainable Development*. Geneva: ITU/Unesco; http://broadbandcommission.org/Documents/reports/bbannual report2016.pdf.

Broadband Commission for Sustainable Development, Unesco and Intel (2017) *Working Group on Education: Digital Skills for Life and Work*. Paris: Unesco; https://unesdoc.unesco.org/ark:/48223/pf0000259013.

Brosnan, M. J. (1998) The impact of computer anxiety and self-efficacy upon performance, *Journal of Computer Assisted Learning*, 14(3): 223–34.

Bruch, E. E., and Mare, R. D. (2008) *Segregation Processes*, working paper, California Center for Population Research; repr. as Segregation dynamics in P. Hedström and P. Bearman (eds) (2009), *The Oxford Handbook of Analytical Sociology*. New York: Oxford University Press, pp. 269–93.

Brundidge, J. (2010) Encountering 'difference' in the contemporary public sphere: the contribution of the internet to the heterogeneity of political discussion networks, *Journal of Communication*, 60(4): 680–700.

Bubaš, G., and Hutinski, Z. (2003) Conceptual model, empirically derived predictors and potential dimensions of internet affinity, manuscript submitted for presentation consideration, University of Zagreb, Croatia.

Büchi, M., Just, N., and Latzer, M. (2016) Modeling the second-level digital divide: a five-country study of social differences in internet use, *New Media & Society*, 18(11): 2703–22.

Buckingham, D. (2008) Introducing identity, in Buckingham (ed.), *Youth, Identity, and Digital Media*. Cambridge, MA: MIT Press, pp. 1–24.

Bunz, U. (2004) The computer-email-web (CEW) fluency scale-development and validation, *International Journal of Human–Computer Interaction*, 17(4): 479–506.

Bunz, U. (2009) A generational comparison of gender, computer anxiety, and computer-email-web fluency, *Studies in Media & Information Literacy Education*, 9(2): 54–69.

Calvani, A., Fini, A., Ranieri, M., and P. Picci (2012) Are young generations in secondary school digitally competent? A study on Italian teenagers, *Computers & Education*, 58(2): 797–807.

Carretero, S., Vuorikari, R., and Punie, Y. (2017) *DigComp 2.1: The Digital Competence Framework for Citizens with Eight Proficiency Levels and Examples of Use*. Luxembourg: Joint Research Centre, European Commission.

Carvin, A., (2000) *More than Just Access: Fitting Literacy and Content into the Digital Divide Equation*, https://er.educause.edu/-/media/files/article-down loads/erm0063.pdf.

Castells, M. (1996) *The Information Age: Economy, Society, and Culture*, Vol. 1: *The Rise of the Network Society*. Oxford: Blackwell.

Chadwick, D., Wesson, C., and Fullwood, C. (2013) Internet access by people with intellectual disabilities: inequalities and opportunities, *Future Internet*, 5(3): 376–97.

Chesley, N., and Johnson, B. E. (2014) Information and communication technology use and social connectedness over the life course, *Sociology Compass*, 8(6): 589–602.

Cho, J., de Zúñiga, H. G., Rojas, H., and Shah, D. V. (2003) Beyond access: the digital divide and internet uses and gratifications, *IT & Society*, 1(4): 46–72.

Chua, S. L., Chen, D.-T., and Wong, A. F. L. (1999) Computer anxiety and its correlates: a meta-analysis, *Computers in Human Behavior*, 15(5): 609–23.

Clark, L. S. (2009) Digital media and the generation gap: qualitative research on US teens and their parents, *Information, Communication & Society*, 12(3): 388–407.

Coleman, J. S. (1990) *Foundations of Social Theory*. Cambridge, MA: Harvard University Press.

Compaine, B. (ed.) (2001) *The Digital Divide: Facing a Crisis or Creating a Myth?* Cambridge, MA: MIT Press.

Correa, T. (2014) Bottom-up technology transmission within families: exploring how youths influence their parents' digital media use with dyadic data, *Journal of Communication*, 64(1): 103–24.

Correa, T., Hinsley, A. W., and de Zúñiga, H. G. (2010) Who interacts on the web? The intersection of users' personality and social media use, *Computers in Human Behavior*, 26(2): 247–53.

Coulangeon, P. (2015) Social mobility and musical tastes: a reappraisal of the social meaning of taste eclecticism, *Poetics*, 51: 54–68.

Courtois, C., and Verdegem, P. (2016) With a little help from my friends: an analysis of the role of social support in digital inequalities, *New Media & Society*, 18(8): 1508–27.

Crabtree, J. (2001) The digital divide is rubbish – a kind of exclusion that shouldn't worry us, *New Statesman*, May 14, p. 26.

Cruz-Jesus, F., Vicente, M., Bacao, F., and Oliveira, T. (2016) The education-related digital divide: an analysis for the EU-28, *Computers in Human Behavior*, 56: 72–82.

Cruz-Jesus, F., Oliveira, T., and Bacao, F. (2018) The global digital divide: evidence and drivers, *Journal of Global Information Management*, 26(2): 1–26.

Cullen, R., and Morse, S. (2011) Who's contributing: do personality traits influence the level and type of participation in online communities? *44th Hawaii International Conference on System Sciences*, January 4–7.

Davies, H. C., and Eynon, R. (2018) Is digital upskilling the next generation our "pipeline to prosperity"?, *New Media & Society*, 20(11): 3961–79.

Davis, F. D. (1989) Perceived usefulness, perceived ease of use, and user acceptance of information technology, *MIS Quarterly*, 13(3): 319–40.

Dhir, A., Chen, S., and Nieminen, M. (2016) The effects of demographics, technology accessibility, and unwillingness to communicate in predicting Internet gratifications and heavy Internet use among adolescents, *Social Science Computer Review*, 34(3): 278–97.

Digital Economy and Society Index (DESI) (2018) Brussels: European Commission, https://ec.europa.eu/digital-single-market/en/desi.

Digital Inclusion Research Group (2017) *Digital New Zealanders: The Pulse of our Nation*. Wellington: Ministry of Business Innovation and Employment, https://2020.org.nz/blog/2017/12/06/digital-divide-pulse-our-nation/.

DiMaggio, P., and Garip, F. (2012) Network effects and social inequality, *Annual Review of Sociology*, 38: 93–118.

DiMaggio, P., Hargittai, E., Celeste, C., and Shafer, S. (2004) Digital inequality: from unequal access to differentiated use, in K. M. Neckerman (ed.), *Social Inequality*. New York: Russell Sage Foundation, pp. 355–400.

Dobransky, K., and Hargittai, E. (2016) Unrealized potential: exploring the digital disability divide, *Poetics*, 58: 18–28.

Donner, J., Gitau, S., and Marsden, G. (2011) Exploring mobile-only Internet use: results of a training study in urban South Africa, *International Journal of Communication*, 5: 574–97.

Draper, H. (1978) *Karl Marx's Theory of Revolution*, Vol. 2: *The Politics of Social Classes*. New York: Monthly Review Press.

Duggan, M. (2017) *Online Harassment 2017*. Washington, DC: Pew Research Center.

Duplaga, M. (2017) Digital divide among people with disabilities: analysis of data from a nationwide study for determinants of internet use and activities performed online, *PloS One*, 12(6): 1–19.

Dutton, W. H., and Reisdorf, B. C. (2017) Cultural divides and digital inequalities: attitudes shaping internet and social media divides, *Information, Communication & Society*, 22(1): 18–38.

Dyson, E. (1997) *Release 2.0: A Design for Living in the Digital Age*. New York: Broadway Books.

The Economist Intelligence Unit (2019) *The Inclusive Internet Index 2018*, https://theinclusiveinternet.eiu.com/assets/external/downloads/3i-executive-summary.pdf.

Ecorys and DTI (Danish Technological Institute) (2016) *ICT for Work: Digital Skills in the Workplace. The Impact of ICT on Job Quality: Evidence from 12 Job Profiles*. Luxembourg: European Union.

Ellison, N. B., Steinfield, C., and Lampe, C. (2011) Connection strategies: social capital implications of Facebook-enabled communication practices, *New Media & Society*, 13(6): 873–92.

ETNO (European Telecommunications Network Operators' Association) (2016) *Annual Economic Report*. Brussels: ETNO; https://etno.eu/datas/publications/economic-reports/ETNO%20Annual%20Economic%20Report%202016.pdf.

ETNO (European Telecommunications Network Operators' Association) (2017) *Annual Economic Report*. Brussels: ETNO; https://etno.eu/datas/publications/annual-reports/ETNO%20Annual%20Economic%20Report%202017%20(final%20version%20web).pdf.

European Commission (1996) *Communication ... on Universal Service for Telecommunications*, COM (96)73 (12 March). Brussels: European Commission.

European Commission (2016a) *Connectivity for a Competitive Digital Single Market – Towards a European Gigabit Society, SWD(2016), 300 final*. Brussels: European Commission.

European Commission (2016b) *A New Skills Agenda for Europe: Working Together to Strengthen Human Capital, Employability and Competitiveness, COM(2016) 381 final*. Brussels: European Commission.

Falck, O., Heimisch, A., and Wiederhold, S. (2016) *Returns to ICT Skills*, OECD Education Working Paper no. 134.

Ferrant, C. (2018) Class, culture, and structure: stratification and mechanisms of omnivorousness, *Sociology Compass*, 12(7): 1–12.

Festinger, L. (1954) A theory of social comparison processes, *Human relations*, 7(2): 117–40.

Finn, S., and Korukonda, A. R. (2004) Avoiding computers: does personality play a role?, in E. P. Bucy and J. E. Newhagen (eds), *Media Access: Social and Psychological Dimensions of New Technology Use*. Mahwah, NJ: Lawrence Erlbaum Associates, pp. 73–90.

Fischer, C. S., Hout, M., Sánchez Jankowski, M., Lucas, S. R., Swidler, A., and Voss, K. (1996) *Inequality by Design: Cracking the Bell Curve Myth*. Princeton, NJ: Princeton University Press.

Flanagan, D. P., and Harrison, P. L. (eds) (2012) *Contemporary Intellectual Assessment: Theories, Tests, and Issues*. 3rd edn, New York: Guilford Press.

Flanagin, A. J., and Metzger, M. J. (2001) Internet use in the contemporary media environment, *Human Communication Research*, 27(1): 153–81.

Fox, S. (2011) *Americans Living with Disability and Their Technology Profile*. Washington, DC: Pew Internet & American Life Project.

Fox, S., and Duggan, M. (2013) *Health Online 2013*. Washington, DC: Pew Research Center.

Fuchs, C. (2009) The role of income inequality in a multivariate cross-national analysis of the digital divide, *Social Science Computer Review*, 27(1): 41–58.

Gaschet, F., and Gallo, J. L. (2005) The spatial dimension of segregation: a case study in four urban areas, 1990–1999, paper presented at the 45th congress of the European Regional Science Association: "Land use and water management in a sustainable network society", Amsterdam, August 23–7.

Gates, B. (2000) Keynote address to the 'Creating Digital Dividends' conference, Seattle, 18 October, https://voicesofdemocracy.umd.edu/gates-keynote-address-speech-text/.

Gerber, A. S., Huber, G. A., Doherty, D., and Dowling, C. M. (2011) Personality traits and the consumption of political information, *American Politics Research*, 39(1): 32–84.

Giddens, A. (1984) *The Constitution of Society: Outline of the Theory of Structuration*. Cambridge: Polity.

Giddens, A. (1991) *Modernity and Self-Identity: Self and Society in the Late Modern Age*. Cambridge: Polity.

Gilster, P. (1997) *Digital Literacy*. Chichester: Wiley.

Goldthorpe, J., Llewellyn C., and Payne, C. (1987) *Social Mobility and Class Structure in Modern Britain*. 2nd edn, Oxford: Clarendon Press.

Gonzales, A. (2014) Health benefits and barriers to cell phone use in low-income urban U.S. neighborhoods: indications of technology maintenance, *Mobile Media & Communication*, 2(3): 233–48.

Gonzales, A. (2016) The contemporary US digital divide: from initial access to technology maintenance, *Information, Communication & Society*, 19(2): 234–48.

Gordon, R. J. (2016) *The Rise and Fall of American Growth: The U.S. Standard of Living since the Civil War*. Princeton, NJ: Princeton University Press.

Graham, S., and Thrift, N. (2007) Out of order: understanding repair and maintenance, *Theory, Culture & Society*, 24(3): 1–25.

Granovetter, M. (1983) The strength of weak ties: a network theory revisited, *Sociological theory*, 1: 201–33.

Gui, M., and Argentin, G. (2011) Digital skills of internet natives: different forms of digital literacy in a random sample of northern Italian high school students, *New Media & Society*, 13(6): 963–80.

Guilford, J. P. (1967) *The Nature of Human Intelligence*. New York: McGraw-Hill.

Gunkel, D. J. (2003) Second thoughts: toward a critique of the digital divide, *New Media & Society*, 5(4): 499–522.

Gutiérrez, P., and Martorell, A. (2011) People with intellectual disability and ICTs, *Revista comunicar*, 18(36): 173–80.

Hale, T. M. (2013) Is there such a thing as an online health lifestyle? Examining the relationship between social status, internet access, and health behaviors, *Information, Communication & Society*, 16(4): 501–18.

Hamburger, Y. A., and Ben-Artzi, E. (2000) The relationship between extraversion and neuroticism and the different uses of the internet, *Computers in Human Behavior*, 16(4): 441–9.

Harari, Y. N. (2016) *Homo Deus: A Brief History of Tomorrow*. New York: Random House.

Harari, Y. N. (2018) *21 Lessons for the 21st Century*. London: Jonathan Cape.

Hargittai, E. (2002) The second-level digital divide: differences in people's online skills, First Monday, 7(4), https://firstmonday.org/ajs/index.php/fm/issue/view/144.

Hargittai, E. (2010) Digital na(t)ives? Variation in Internet skills and uses among members of the 'net generation', *Sociological Inquiry*, 80(1): 92–113.

Hargittai, E., and Dobransky, K. (2017) Old dogs, new clicks: digital inequality in skills and uses among older adults, *Canadian Journal of Communication*, 42(2): 195–212.

Hargittai, E., and Hinnant, A. (2008) Digital inequality: differences in young adults' use of the internet, *Communication Research*, 35(5): 602–21.

Hargittai, E., and Kim, S. J. (2010) *The Prevalence of Smartphone Use among a Wired Group of Young Adults*, working paper, Institute for Policy Research, Northwestern University.

Hargittai, E., and Shafer, S. (2006) Differences in actual and perceived online skills: the role of gender, *Social Science Quarterly*, 87(2): 432–48.

Helsper, E. J. (2012) A corresponding fields model for the links between social and digital exclusion, *Communication Theory*, 22(4): 403–26.

Helsper, E. J., and Eynon, R. (2010) Digital natives: where is the evidence?, *British Educational Research Journal*, 36(3): 503–20.

Helsper, E. J., and Galácz, A. (2009) Understanding the links between social and digital inclusion in Europe, in G. Cardoso, A. Cheong and J. Cole (eds), *World Wide Internet: Changing Societies, Economies and Cultures*. Taipa: University of Macau Press, pp. 146–178.

Helsper, E. J., and Reisdorf, B. C. (2017) The emergence of a "digital underclass" in Great Britain and Sweden: changing reasons for digital exclusion, *New Media & Society*, 19(8): 1253–70.

Helsper, E. J., and van Deursen, A. J. (2015) Digital skills in Europe: research and policy, in K. Andreasson (ed.), *Digital Divides: The New Challenges and Opportunities of e-Inclusion*. Boca Raton, FL: CRC Press, pp. 126–46.

Helsper, E. J., and van Deursen, A. J. (2017) Do the rich get digitally richer? Quantity and quality of support for digital engagement, *Information, Communication & Society*, 20(5): 700–14.

Helsper, E. J., van Deursen, A. J., and Eynon, R. (2015) *Tangible Outcomes of Internet Use: From Digital Skills to Tangible Outcomes Project Report*. Oxford: Oxford Internet Institute.

Hilbert, M. (2011a) Digital gender divide or technologically empowered women in developing countries? A typical case of lies, damned lies, and statistics, *Women's Studies International Forum*, 34(6): 479–89.

Hilbert, M. (2011b) The end justifies the definition: the manifold outlooks on the digital divide and their practical usefulness for policy-making, *Telecommunications Policy*, 35(8): 715–36.

Hilbert, M. (2016) The bad news is that the digital access divide is here to stay: domestically installed bandwidths among 172 countries for 1986–2014, *Telecommunications Policy*, 40(6): 567–81.

Hilbert, M., López, P., and Vásquez, C. (2010) Information societies or "ICT equipment societies?" Measuring the digital information-processing capacity of a society in bits and bytes, *Information Society*, 26(3): 157–78.

Hilferding, R. (1981) *Finance Capital: A Study of the Latest Phase of Capitalist Development*. London: Routledge & Kegan Paul.

Hirsch, F. (1976) *The Social Limits to Growth*. London: Routledge & Kegan Paul.

Hobbs, R. (2011) *Digital and Media Literacy: Connecting Culture and Classroom*. Thousand Oaks, CA: Corwin Press.

Hoffman, D. L., Novak, T. P., and Schlosser, A. (2000) The evolution of the digital divide: how gaps in internet access may impact electronic commerce, *Journal of Computer-Mediated Communication*, 5(3): JCMC534.

Hofstra, B., Corten, R., van Tubergen, F., and Ellison, N. B. (2017) Sources of segregation in social networks: a novel approach using Facebook, *American Sociological Review*, 82(3): 625–56.

Horrigan, J. B. (2000) *New Internet Users: What They Do Online, What They Don't, and Implications for the Net's Future*. Washington, DC: Pew Internet & American Life Project.

Horrigan, J. B. (2016) *Information Overload*. Washington DC: Pew Research Center.

Horrigan, J. B. (2017) *How People Approach Facts and Information*. Washington, DC: Pew Research Center.

Horrigan, J., and Duggan, M. (2015) *Home Broadband 2015*. Washington, DC: Pew Research Center.

Hudiburg, R. A., Pashaj, I., and Wolfe, R. (1999) Preliminary investigation of computer stress and the big five personality factors, *Psychology Reports*, 85(2): 473–80.

IMDA (Infocomm Media Development Authority) (2018) *Digital Economy Framework for Action*, www.imda.gov.sg/sgdigital/digital-economy-framework-for-action.

Ito, M., Horst, H., Bittanti, M., boyd, d., Herr-Stephenson, Lange, P. G., Pascoe, C. J., and Robinson, L. (2009) *Living and Learning with New Media: Summary of Findings from the Digital Youth Project*. Cambridge, MA: MIT Press.

ITU (International Telecommunication Union) (2017) *Measuring the Information Society Report*, Vol. 1. Geneva: ITU.

Jackson, L. A., Ervin, K. S., Gardner, P. D., and Schmitt, N. (2001) Gender and the internet: women communicating and men searching, *Sex Roles*, 44(5–6): 363–79.

James, J. (2003) *Technology, Globalization and Poverty*. Cheltenham: Edward Elgar.

James, J. (2008) Digital divide complacency: misconceptions and dangers, *Information Society*, 24(1): 54–61.

Jorba, L., and Bimber, B. (2012) The impact of digital media on citizenship from a global perspective, in E. Anduiza, M. Jensen, and L. Jorba (eds), *Digital Media and Political Engagement Worldwide: A Comparative Study*. New York: Cambridge University Press, pp. 16–38.

KADO (Korea Agency for Digital Opportunity and Promotion) (2003) *Bridging the Digital Divide*. Seoul: KADO.

Kadushin, C. (2012) *Understanding Social Networks: Theories, Concepts and Findings*. New York: Oxford University Press.

Kalmus, V., Realo, A., and Siibak, A. (2011) Motives for internet use and their relationships with personality traits and socio-demographic factors, *Trames*, 15(4): 385–403.

Karlsen, R., Steen-Johnsen, K., Wollebæk, D., and Enjolras, B. (2017) Echo chamber and trench warfare dynamics in online debates, *European Journal of Communication*, 32(3): 257–73.

Katz, E., Blumler, J. G., and Gurevitch, M. (1973) Uses and gratifications research, *Public Opinion Quarterly*, 37(4): 509–23.

Katz, J. E. (2006) *Magic in the Air: Mobile Communication and the Transformation of Social Life*. New Brunswick, NJ: Transaction.

Katz, J. E., and Rice, R. E. (2002) *Social Consequences of Internet Use: Access, Involvement, and Interaction*. Cambridge, MA: MIT Press.

Landers, R. N., and Lounsbury, J. W. (2006) An investigation of big five and narrow personality traits in relation to internet usage, *Computers in Human Behavior*, 22(2): 283–93.

LaRose, R., and Eastin, M. S. (2004) A social cognitive theory of internet uses and gratifications: toward a new model of media attendance, *Journal of Broadcasting & Electronic Media*, 48(3): 358–77.

Leander, K. (2007) "You won't be needing your laptops today": wired bodies in the wireless classroom, in M. Knobel and C. Lankshear (eds), *A New Literacies Sampler*. New York: Peter Lang, pp. 25–48.

Lee, J. J., Wedow, R., Okbay, A., et al. (2018) Gene discovery and polygenic prediction from a genome-wide association study of educational attainment in 1.1 million individuals, *Nature Genetics*, 50: 1112–21.

Lee, J. K., Choi, J., Kim, C., and Kim, Y. (2014) Social media, network heterogeneity, and opinion polarization, *Journal of Communication*, 64(4): 702–22.

Lenhart, A. (2000) *Who's Not Online: 57% of Those without Internet Access Say They Do Not Plan to Log On*. Washington, DC: Pew Internet & American Life Project.

Lenhart, A., Horrigan, J., Rainie, L., Allen, K., Boyce, A., Madden, M., and O'Grady, E. (2003) *The Ever-Shifting Internet Population: A New Look at Internet Access and the Digital Divide*. Washington DC: Pew Internet & American Life Project.

Levine, L., and Taylor, M. P. H. (2018) *Closing the Digital Divide: A Historic and Economic Justification for Government Intervention*, working paper, UC Riverside, School of Public Policy.

Lindblom, T., and Räsänen, P. (2017) Between class and status? Examining the digital divide in Finland, the United Kingdom, and Greece, *Information Society*, 33(3): 147–58.

Litt, E. (2013) Measuring users' internet skills: a review of past assessments and a look toward the future, *New Media & Society*, 15(4): 612–30.

Littler, J. (2018) *Against Meritocracy: Culture, Power and Myths of Mobility*. Abingdon: Routledge.

Livingstone, S., and Helsper, E. (2007) Gradations in digital inclusion: children, young people and the digital divide, *New Media & Society*, 9(4): 671–96.

Livingstone, S., and Helsper, E. (2010) Balancing opportunities and risks in teenagers' use of the Internet: the role of online skills and Internet self-efficacy, *New Media & Society*, 12(2): 309–29.

Livingstone, S., Van Couvering, E., and Thumim, N. (2005) Adult media literacy: a review of the research literature, https://dera.ioe.ac.uk/5283/1/aml.pdf.

Loos, E. (2012) Senior citizens: digital immigrants in their own country? *Observatorio (OBS*) Journal*, 6(1): 1–23.

Lyon, D. (1988) *The Information Society: Issues and Illusions*. Cambridge: Polity.

McNamee, S. J., and Miller, R. K. (2009) *The Meritocracy Myth*. Lanham, MD: Rowman & Littlefield.

Madden, M., and L. Rainie (2003) *America's Online Pursuits: The Changing Picture of Who's Online and What They Do*. Washington, DC: Pew Internet & American Life Project.

Mallett, A., Stephens, J. C., Wilson, E. J., Langheim, R., Reiber, R., and Peterson, T. R. (2017) Electric (dis)connections: comparative review of smart grid news coverage in the United States and Canada, *Renewable and Sustainable Energy Reviews*, 82(2): 1913–21.

Mansell, R. (2002) From digital divides to digital entitlements in knowledge societies, *Current Sociology*, 50(3): 407–26.

Mansell, R., and When, U. (1998) *Knowledge Societies: Information Technology for Sustainable Development*. Oxford: Oxford University Press.

Mariën, I., and Prodnik, J. A. (2014) Digital inclusion and user (dis)empowerment: a critical perspective, *Info*, 16(6): 35–47.

Martínez-Cantos, J. L. (2017). Digital skills gaps: a pending subject for gender digital inclusion in the European Union, *European Journal of Communication*, 32(5): 419–38.

Maslow, A. H. (1943) A theory of human motivation, *Psychological Review*, 50(4): 370–96.

Mesch, G. S., and Talmud, I. (2011) Ethnic differences in internet access, *Information, Communication & Society*, 14(4): 445–71.

Michaels, G., Natraj, A., and Van Reenen, J. (2014) Has ICT polarized skill demand? Evidence from eleven countries over 25 years, *Review of Economics and Statistics*, 96(1): 60–77.

Milanovic, B. (2016) *Global Inequality: A New Approach for the Age of Globalization*. Cambridge, MA: Harvard University Press.

Milgram, S. (1967) The small-world problem, *Psychology Today*, 1(1): 61–7.

Monge, P. R., and Contractor, N. S. (2003) *Theories of Communication Networks*. New York: Oxford University Press.

Mossberger, K., Tolbert, C., and Stansbury, M. (2003) *Virtual Inequality: Beyond the Digital Divide*. Washington, DC: Georgetown University Press.

Mossberger, K., Tolbert, C. J., and Hamilton, A. (2012) Measuring digital citizenship: mobile access and broadband, *International Journal of Communication*, 6: 2492–528.

Mossberger, K., Tolbert, C. J., and Anderson, C. (2014) Digital citizenship: broadband, mobile use, and activities online, *Proceedings of the International Political Science Association Conference*, Montreal, July.

Mounk, Y. (2018) *The People vs. Democracy: Why Our Freedom is in Danger and How to Save it*. Cambridge, MA: Harvard University Press.

Murphy, H. C., Chen, M.-M., and Cossutta, M. (2016) An investigation of multiple devices and information sources used in the hotel booking process, *Tourism Management*, 52: 44–51.

Musterd, S., Marcińczak, S., van Ham, M., and Tammaru, T. (2017) Socioeconomic segregation in European capital cities: increasing separation between poor and rich, *Urban Geography*, 38(7): 1062–83.

Mutsvairo, B., and Ragnedda, M. (2019) *Mapping Digital Divide in Africa: A Mediated Analysis*. New York: Routledge.

Mwim, E. N., and Kritzinger, E. (2016) Digital divide, the role of awareness in the use/non-use of the internet: the experience of South African developing communities, *Proceedings of the African Cybercitizenship Conference*, Port Elizabeth, South Africa, 31 October – 1 November.

Nahuis, R., and de Groot, H. L. F. (2003) *Rising Skills Premia: You Ain't Seen Nothing Yet*, CPB Discussion Paper No. 20.

Naisbitt, J. (1982) *Megatrends: Ten New Directions Transforming Our Lives*. London: Macdonald.

Napoli, P. M., and Obar, J. A. (2014) The emerging mobile internet underclass: a critique of mobile internet access, *Information Society*, 30(5): 323–34.

Napoli, P. M., and Obar, J. A. (2017) Second class netizens: race and the emerging mobile Internet underclass, in R. A. Lind (ed.), *Race and Gender in Electronic Media: Content, Context, Culture*. New York: Routledge, pp. 293–311.

Negroponte, N. (1995) *Being Digital*. New York: Knopf.

Nie, N. H., and Erbring, L. (2002) Internet and society: a preliminary report, *IT & Society*, 1(1): 275–83.

Nielsen, J. (1994) *Usability Engineering*. San Francisco: Morgan Kaufmann.

Nishijima, M., Ivanauskas, T. M., and Sarti, F. M. (2017) Evolution and determinants of digital divide in Brazil (2005–2013), *Telecommunications Policy*, 41(1): 12–24.

Norris, P. (2001) *Digital Divide: Civic Engagement, Information Poverty, and the Internet Worldwide*. Cambridge: Cambridge University Press.

NTIA (National Telecommunications and Information Administration) (1995)

Falling through the Net: A Survey of the 'Have Nots' in Rural And Urban America, www.ntia.doc.gov/ntiahome/fallingthru.html.

NTIA (National Telecommunications and Information Administration) (1998) *Falling through the Net II: New Data on the Digital Divide*, www.ntia.doc.gov/ntiahome/net2/.

NTIA (National Telecommunications and Information Administration) (1999) *Falling through the Net III: Defining the Digital Divide*, www.ntia.doc.gov/ntiahome/fttn99/part1.html.

NTIA (National Telecommunications and Information Administration) (2000) *Falling through the Net: Toward Digital Inclusion*, www.ntia.doc.gov/ntiahome/fttn00/contents00.html.

NTIA (National Telecommunications and Information Administration) (2002) *A Nation Online: How Americans Are Expanding Their Use of the Internet*, www.ntia.doc.gov/legacy/ntiahome/dn/nationonline_020502.htm.

NTIA (National Telecommunications and Information Administration) (2009) *Broadband USA: Connecting America's Communities*, www2.ntia.doc.gov/.

NTIA (National Telecommunications and Information Administration) (2013) *Exploring the Digital Nation: America's Emerging Online Experience*, www.ntia.doc.gov/files/ntia/publications/exploring_the_digital_nation_-_americas_emerging_online_experience.pdf.

OECD (2010) *Sickness Disability and Work: Breaking the Barriers*. Paris: OECD.

Ofcom (2015) *Disabled Consumers' Use of Communications Services: A Consumer Experience Report*, http://stakeholders.ofcom.org.uk/binaries/research/media-literacy/1515282/Disabled_consumers_use_of_communications_services.pdf.

Oggolder, C. (2015) From virtual to social: transforming concepts and images of the internet, *Information & Culture*, 50(2): 181–96.

Olmstead, K., and Smith, A. (2017a) *Americans and Cybersecurity*. Washington, DC: Pew Research Center.

Olmstead, K., and Smith, A. (2017b) *What the Public Knows about Cybersecurity*. Washington, DC: Pew Research Center.

Ostendorf, W., Musterd, S., and de Vos, S. (2001) Social mix and neighbourhood effect: policy ambitions and empirical evidence, *Housing Studies*, 16(3): 371–80.

Papacharissi, Z., and Rubin, A. (2000) Predictors of internet use, *Journal of Broadcasting & Electronic Media*, 44(2): 175–96.

Pariser, E. (2011) *The Filter Bubble: What the Internet is Hiding from You*. London: Penguin.

Park, H. W. (2002) The digital divide in South Korea: closing and widening divides in the 1990s, http://unpan1.un.org/intradoc/groups/public/documents/apcity/unpan046433.pdf.

Park, S. (2017) The state of digital inequalities: interplay between social and digital exclusion, in Park, *Digital Capital*. Basingstoke: Palgrave Macmillan, pp. 35–62.

Park, S., and Kim, G. J. (2014) Lessons from South Korea's digital divide index (DDI), *Info*, 16(3): 72–84.

Partnership for 21st Century Skills (2008) *21st Century Skills, Education &*

Competitiveness: A Resource and Policy Guide, https://files.eric.ed.gov/fulltext/ED519337.pdf.

Pearce, K. E., and Rice, R. E. (2013) Digital divides from access to activities: comparing mobile and personal computer internet users, *Journal of Communication*, 63(4): 721–44.

Peña-López, I. (2009) *Measuring Digital Development for Policy-Making: Models, Stages, Characteristics and Causes*, Ph.D thesis, Barcelona: Universitat Oberta de Catalunya.

Perrin, A., and Duggan, M. (2015) *Americans' Internet Access: 2000–2015.* Washington, DC: Pew Research Center.

Peterson, R. A. (1992) Understanding audience segmentation: from elite and mass to omnivore and univore, *Poetics*, 21(4): 243–58.

Pew Research Center (2018) Internet/broadband fact sheet, www.pewinternet.org/fact-sheet/internet-broadband/.

Pick, J., and Sarkar, A. (2015) *The Global Digital Divides: Explaining Change.* Heidelberg: Springer.

Piketty, T. (2014) *Capital in the Twenty-First Century.* Cambridge, MA: Harvard University Press.

Potter, W. J. ([1998] 2008) *Media Literacy.* 4th edn, Thousand Oaks, CA: Sage.

Poushter, J., Bishop, C., and Chwe, H. (2018) *Social Media Use Continues to Rise in Developing Countries but Plateaus across Developed Ones.* Washington, DC: Pew Research Center.

Prensky, M. (2001) Digital natives, digital immigrants, *On the Horizon*, 9(5):1–6.

Putnam, R. D. (2000) Bowling alone: America's declining social capital, in L. Crothers and C. Lockhart (eds), *Culture and Politics: A Reader.* New York: Palgrave Macmillan, pp. 223–34.

Quan-Haase, A., and Wellman, B., with Witte, J. C., and Hampton, K. N. (2002) Capitalizing on the net: social contact, civic engagement, and sense of community, in B. Wellman and C. Haythornthwaite (eds), *The Internet in Everyday Life.* Oxford: Blackwell, pp. 291–324.

Ragnedda, M. (2017) *The Third Digital Divide: A Weberian Approach to Digital Inequalities.* New York: Routledge.

Ragnedda, M., and Muschert, G. W. (eds) (2013) *The Digital Divide: The Internet and Social Inequality in International Perspective.* New York: Routledge.

Rainie, L., and Wellman, B. (2012) *Networked.* Cambridge, MA: MIT Press.

Rappoport, P., Alleman, J., and Madden, G. (2009) A cross-country assessment of the digital divide, in B. Preissl, J. Haucap and P. Curwen (eds), *Telecommunication Markets: Drivers and Impediments.* Heidelberg: Physica, pp. 433–47.

Reed, D., Haroon, J., and Ryan, P. S. (2014) Technologies and policies to connect the next five billion, *Berkeley Technology Law Journal*, 29(2): 1205–52.

Reisdorf, B. C., and Groselj, D. (2017) Internet (non-)use types and motivational access: implications for digital inequalities research, *New Media & Society*, 19(8): 1157–76.

Reisdorf, B. C., Triwibowo, W., Nelson, M., and Dutton, W. (2017) An interrupted history of digital divides, Paper presented at the 17th annual meeting of the Association of Internet Researchers, Berlin.

Rheingold, H. (1993) *The Virtual Community: Homesteading on the Electronic Frontier.* Reading, MA: Addison-Wesley.

Robinson, L. (2009) A taste for the necessary: a Bourdieuian approach to digital inequality, *Information, Communication & Society*, 12(4): 488–507.

Robinson, L., Cotten, S. R., Ono, H., Quan-Haase, A., Mesch, G., Chen, W., Schulz, J., Hale, T. M., and Stern, M. J. (2015) Digital inequalities and why they matter, *Information, Communication & Society*, 18(5): 569–82.

Robles, J. M., and Molina, Ó. (2007) La brecha digital: ¿una consecuencia más de las desigualdades sociales? Un análisis de caso para Andalucía, *Empiria: revista de metodología de ciencias sociales*, no. 13: 81–99.

Robles, J. M., and Torres Albero, C. (2012) Digital divide and the information and communication society in Spain, *Journal for Spatial and Socio-Cultural Development Studies*, 50(3): 291–307.

Robles Morales, J. M., Torres Albero, C., and Molina, Ó. M. (2010) La brecha digital: un análisis de las desigualdades tecnológicas en España, *Sistema: revista de ciencias sociales*, 218: 3–22.

Robles, J. M., Molina, Ó., and De Marco, S. (2012) Participación política digital y brecha digital política en España: un estudio de las desigualdades digitales, *Arbor*, 188: 795–810.

Rogers, E. M. ([1962] 2003) *Diffusion of Innovations.* 5th edn, New York: Free Press.

Rosen, L. D. (2012) *iDisorder: Understanding our Obsession with Technology and Overcoming its Hold on Us.* New York: Palgrave Macmillan.

Rosengren, K. E., Wenner, L. A., and Palmgreen, P. (eds) (1985) *Media Gratifications Research: Current Perspectives.* Beverly Hills CA: Sage.

Rubio, E., Rinaldi, D., and Pellerin-Carlin, T. (2016) *Investment in Europe: Making the Best of the Juncker Plan.* Paris: Jacques Delors Institute.

Russo, S., and Amnå, E. (2016) The personality divide: do personality traits differentially predict online political engagement?, *Social Science Computer Review*, 34(3): 259–77.

Ryan, C., and Lewis, J. M. (2017) *Computer and Internet Use in the United States: 2015.* Washington, DC: United States Census Bureau.

Ryan, T., and Xenos, S. (2011) Who uses Facebook? An investigation into the relationship between the Big Five, shyness, narcissism, loneliness, and Facebook usage, *Computers in Human Behavior*, 27(5): 1658–64.

Salemink, K., Strijker, D., and Bosworth, G. (2017) Rural development in the digital age: a systematic literature review on unequal ICT availability, adoption, and use in rural areas, *Journal of Rural Studies*, 54: 360–71.

Savage, M., Devine, F., Cunningham, N., Taylor, M., Li, Y., Hjellbrekke, J., Le Roux, B., Friedman, S., and Miles, A. (2013) A new model of social class? Findings from the BBC's Great British Class Survey experiment, *Sociology*, 47(2): 219–50.

Scheerder, A., van Deursen, A., and van Dijk, J. (2017) Determinants of internet skills, uses and outcomes: a systematic review of the second- and third-level digital divide, *Telematics and Informatics*, 34(8): 1607–24.

Schiller, H. I. (1981) *Who Knows: Information in the Age of the Fortune 500*. Norwood, NJ: Ablex.

Schiller, H. I. (1996) *Information Inequality: The Deepening Social Crisis in America*. New York: Routledge.

Schoemaker, E. (2014) The mobile web: amplifying, but not creating, changemakers, *Innovations*, 9(3–4): 75–85.

Schumacher, P., and Morahan-Martin, J. (2001) Gender, internet and computer attitudes and experiences, *Computers in Human Behavior*, 17(1): 95–110.

Selwyn, N. (2004) Reconsidering political and popular understandings of the digital divide, *New Media & Society*, 6(3): 341–62.

Selwyn, N. (2003) Apart from technology: understanding people's non-use of information and communication technologies in everyday life, *Technology in Society*, 25(1): 99–116.

Selwyn, N. (2013) *Education in a Digital World: Global Perspectives on Technology and Education*. New York: Routledge.

Selwyn, N., Gorard, S., and Furlong, J. (2006) Adults' use of computers and the internet for self-education, *Studies in the Education of Adults*, 38(2): 141–59.

Sen, A. (1985) *Commodities and Capabilities*. Amsterdam: North-Holland.

Sen, A. (1992) *Inequality Reexamined*. Oxford: Oxford University Press.

Serrano-Cinca, C., Muñoz-Soro, J. F., and Brusca, I. (2018) A multivariate study of internet use and the digital divide, *Social Science Quarterly*, 99(4): 1409–25.

Servaes, J., and Burgelman, J.-C. (2000) The socio-cultural consequences of the European information society, *Telematics and Informatics*, 17(1–2): 1–7.

Servon, L. J. (2002) Redefining the digital divide, *Bridging the Digital Divide: Technology, Community, and Public Policy*. Oxford: Blackwell, pp. 1–23.

Shambaugh, D. (2016) *China's Future*. Cambridge: Polity.

Shenglin, B., Bosc, R., Jiao, J., Li, W., Simonelli, F., and Zhang, R. (2017) *Digital Infrastructure: Overcoming the Digital Divide in China and the European Union*. Brussels: Centre for European Policy Studies.

Shin, D.-H. (2007) A critique of Korean National Information Strategy: case of national information infrastructures, *Government Information Quarterly*, 24(3): 624–45.

Shneiderman, B. (1980) *Software Psychology: Human Factors in Computer and Information Systems*. Cambridge, MA: Winthrop.

Silverstone R., and Hirsch, E. (eds) (1992) *Consuming Technologies: Media and Information in Domestic Spaces*. New York: Routledge.

Silverstone, R., and Mansell, R. (1996) The politics of information and communication technologies, in Mansell and Silverstone (eds), *Communication by Design: The Politics of Information and Communication Technologies*. Oxford: Oxford University Press, pp. 213–28.

Skaletsky, M., Pick, J. B., Sarkar, A., and Yates, D. (2017) Digital divides: past, present, and future, in R. D. Galliers and M. K. Stein (eds), *The Routledge Companion to Management Information Systems*. New York: Routledge; https://inspire.redlands.edu/oh_chapters/58.

Skopek, J., Schulz, F., and Blossfeld, H.-P. (2010) Who contacts whom? Educational homophily in online mate selection, *European Sociological Review*, 27(2): 180–95.

Smith, A. (2013) *Civic Engagement in the Digital Age*. Washington, DC: Pew Research Center.

Smith, A. and Olmstead, K. (2018) *Declining Majority of Online Adults Say the Internet Has Been Good for Society*. Washington, DC: Pew Research Center.

Smith, A., and Page, D. (2016) *15% of American Adults Have Used Online Dating Sites or Mobile Dating Apps*. Washington, DC: Pew Research Center.

Søby, M. (2003) *Digital Competence: From ICT Skills to Digital "Bildung"*. Oslo: University of Oslo Press.

Solomon, G., Allen, N. J., and Resta, P. E. (eds) (2003) *Toward Digital Equity: Bridging the Divide in Education*. Boston: Allyn & Bacon.

Song, I., Larose, R., Eastin, M. S., and Lin, C. A. (2004) Internet gratifications and internet addiction: on the uses and abuses of new media, *CyberPsychology & Behavior*, 7(4): 384–94.

Spitzberg, B. H. (2006) Preliminary development of a model and measure of computer-mediated communication (CMC) competence, *Journal of Computer-Mediated Communication*, 11(2): 629–66.

Spooner, T., and Rainie, H. (2000) *African-Americans and the Internet*. Washington, DC: Pew Internet & American Life Project.

Stafford, T. F., Stafford, M. R., and Schkade, L. L. (2004) Determining uses and gratifications for the internet, *Decision Sciences*, 35(2): 259–88.

Standing, G. (2011) *The Precariat: The New Dangerous Class*. London: Bloomsbury Academic.

Stanley, L. D. (2003) Beyond access: psychosocial barriers to computer literacy. Special issue: ICTs and community networking, *Information Society*, 19(5): 407–16.

Stiglitz, J. E. (2013) *The Price of Inequality: How Today's Divided Society Endangers Our Future*. New York: W. W. Norton.

Sultana, R., and Imtiaz, A. (2018) Gender difference in internet usage pattern: a study on university students of Bangladesh, *Scholars Journal of Economics, Business and Management*, 5(5): 413–21.

Sundar, S. S., and Limperos, A. M. (2013) Uses and grats 2.0: new gratifications for new media, *Journal of Broadcasting & Electronic Media*, 57(4): 504–25.

Sunstein, C. R. (2001) *Republic.com*. Princeton, NJ: Princeton University Press.

Sunstein, C. R. (2008) *Infotopia: How Many Minds Produce Knowledge*. Oxford: Oxford University Press.

Tapscott, D. (1998) *Growing Up Digital: The Rise of the Net Generation*. New York: McGraw-Hill.

Thierer, A. (2000) How free computers are filling the digital divide, *Heritage Foundation Backgrounder*, no. 1361, April 20.

Tichenor, P. J., Donohue, G. A., and Olien, C. N. (1970) Mass media flow and differential growth in knowledge, *Public Opinion Quarterly*, 34(2): 159–70.

Tilly, C. (1998) *Durable Inequality*. Berkeley: University of California Press.

Tobin, C. D. (1983) Developing computer literacy, *Arithmetic Teacher*, 30(6): 22–3.

Tripp, L. M. (2011) 'The computer is not for you to be looking around, it is for schoolwork': challenges for digital inclusion as Latino immigrant families negotiate children's access to the internet, *New Media & Society*, 13(4): 552–67.

Tsetsi, E., and Rains, S. A. (2017) Smartphone internet access and use: extending the digital divide and usage gap, *Mobile Media & Communication*, 5(3): 239–55.

Turner, B. S. (1990) *Theories of Modernity and Postmodernity*. London: Sage.

Tuten, T. L., and Bosnjak, M. (2001) Understanding differences in web usage: the role of need for cognition and the five factor model of personality, *Social Behavior and Personality*, 29(4): 391–8.

Ullah, H., and Ullah, R. (2014) The threatening problem of functional illiteracy: revisiting education, *Social Sciences Review*, 2(2): 1–14.

UNDP (2009) *Human Development Report 2009: Overcoming Barriers: Human Mobility and Development*. New York: United Nations Development Programme.

UNDP (2016) *Human Development Report 2016: Human Development for Everyone*. New York: United Nations Development Programme.

United Nations (2014) *E-Government Survey 2014: E-Government for the Future We Want*. https://publicadministration.un.org/egovkb/portals/egovkb/documents/un/2014-survey/e-gov_complete_survey-2014.pdf.

Urbina, S. (2011) Tests of intelligence, in R. J. Sternberg and S. B. Kaufman (eds), *The Cambridge Handbook of Intelligence*. Cambridge: Cambridge University Press, pp. 20–38.

Valente, T. W. (1996) Network models of the diffusion of innovations, *Computational & Mathematical Organization Theory*, 2(2): 163–4.

van Ark, B., O'Mahony, M., and Timmer, M. P. (2008) The productivity gap between Europe and the United States: trends and causes, *Journal of Economic Perspectives*, 22(1): 25–44.

van Beuningen, J., and Kloosterman, R. (2018) *Opvattingen over sociale media* [Opinions about social media]. The Hague: CBS.

van den Broeck, E., Poels, K., and Walrave, M. (2015) Older and wiser? Facebook use, privacy concern, and privacy protection in the life stages of emerging, young, and middle adulthood, *Social Media & Society*, 1(2): 1–11.

van der Geest, T., van der Meij, H., and van Puffelen, C. (2014) Self-assessed and actual internet skills of people with visual impairments, *Universal Access in the Information Society*, 13(2): 161–74.

van Deursen, A. J. A. M. (2010) *Internet Skills: Vital Assets in an Information Society*, PhD thesis, University of Twente.

van Deursen, A. J. A. M. (2018) *Digitale ongelijkheid in Nederland anno 2018* [Digital inequality in the Netherlands in the year 2018]. Enschede: University of Twente.

van Deursen, A. J. A. M., and Helsper, E. J. (2015) The third-level digital divide: who benefits most from being online? *Studies in Media and Communications*, 10: 29–53.

van Deursen, A. J. A. M., and Helsper, E. J. (2018) Collateral benefits of Internet use: explaining the diverse outcomes of engaging with the Internet, *New Media & Society*, 20(7): 2333–51.

van Deursen, A. J. A. M., and Mossberger, K. (2018) Any thing for anyone? A new digital divide in internet-of-things skills, *Policy & internet*, 10(2): 122–40.

van Deursen, A. J. A. M., and van Dijk, J. A. G. M. (2009) *Trendreport: Motivation, Access, Use and Skills: A European and Dutch Perspective.* Enschede: University of Twente.

van Deursen, A. J. A. M., and van Dijk, J. A. G. M. (2011) Internet skills and the digital divide, *New Media & Society*, 13(6): 893–911.

van Deursen, A. J. A. M., and van Dijk, J. A G. M. (2012) *Trendrapport internetgebruik 2012: een Nederlands en Europees perspectief.* Enschede: University of Twente.

van Deursen, A. J. A. M., and van Dijk, J. A. G. M. (2014a) The digital divide shifts to differences in usage, *New Media & Society*, 16(3): 507–26.

van Deursen, A. J. A. M., and van Dijk, J. A. G. M. (2014b) Loss of labor time due to malfunctioning ICTs and ICT skill insufficiencies, *International Journal of Manpower*, 35(5): 703–19.

van Deursen, A. J. A. M., and van Dijk, J. A. G. M. (2015a) Internet skill levels increase, but gaps widen: a longitudinal cross-sectional analysis (2010–2013) among the Dutch population, *Information, Communication & Society*, 18(7): 782–97.

van Deursen, A. J. A. M., and van Dijk, J. A. G. M. (2015b) Toward a multifaceted model of internet access for understanding digital divides: an empirical investigation, *Information Society*, 31(5): 379–91.

van Deursen, A. J. A. M., and van Dijk, J. A. G. M. (2016) Modeling traditional literacy, internet skills and internet usage: an empirical study, *Interacting with Computers*, 28(1): 13–26.

van Deursen, A. J. A. M., and van Dijk, J. A. G. M. (2019) The first-level digital divide shifts from inequalities in physical access to inequalities in material access, *New Media & Society*, 21(2): 354–75.

van Deursen, A. J. A. M., van Dijk, J. A. G. M., and Peters, O. (2011) Rethinking internet skills: the contribution of gender, age, education, internet experience, and hours online to medium- and content-related internet skills, *Poetics*, 39(2): 125–44.

van Deursen, A. J. A. M., Courtois, C., and van Dijk, J. A. G. M. (2014) Internet skills, sources of support, and benefiting from internet use, *International Journal of Human–Computer Interaction*, 30(4): 278–90.

van Deursen, A. J. A. M., van Dijk, J. A. G. M., and ten Klooster, P. M. (2015) Increasing inequalities in what we do online: a longitudinal cross sectional analysis of internet activities among the Dutch population (2010 to 2013) over gender, age, education, and income, *Telematics and Informatics*, 32(2): 259–72.

van Deursen, A. J. A. M., ben Allouch, S., and Ruijter, L. (2016) Tablet use in primary education: adoption hurdles and attitude determinants, *Education and Information Technologies*, 21(5): 971–90.

van Deursen, A. J. A. M., Helsper, E. J., Eynon, R., and van Dijk, J. A. G. M. (2017) The compoundness and sequentiality of digital inequality, *International Journal of Communication*, 11: 452–73.

van Deursen, A., van der Zeeuw, A., de Boer, P., Jansen, G., and van Rompay, T. (2018) *Gebruik van Internet of Things in Nederland anno 2018* [Usage of the Internet of Things in the Netherlands in 2018]. Enschede: University of Twente.

van Dijk, J. A. G. M. (2000) Widening information gaps and policies of prevention, in K. L. Hacker and J. A. G. M. van Dijk (eds), *Digital Democracy: Issues of Theory and Practice*. Thousand Oaks, CA: Sage, pp. 166–83.

van Dijk, J. A. G. M. ([1991] 2001) *De Netwerkmaatschappij: sociale aspecten van nieuwe media*. 4th edn, Alphen aan den Rijn: Samsom.

van Dijk, J. A. G. M. (2003) *De digitale kloof wordt dieper* [The digital divide is getting deeper]. Amsterdam: SQM and Infodrome@United Knowledge.

van Dijk, J. A. G. M. (2004) Divides in succession: possession, skills and use of new media for societal participation, in E. P. Bucy and J. E. Newhagen (eds), *Media Access: Social and Psychological Dimensions of New Technology Use*. Mahwah, NJ: Lawrence Erlbaum, pp. 233–54.

van Dijk, J. A. G. M. (2005) *The Deepening Divide: Inequality in the Information Society*. Thousand Oaks, CA: Sage.

van Dijk, J. A. G. M. (2006) Digital divide research, achievements and shortcomings, *Poetics*, 34(4–5): 221–35.

van Dijk, J. A. G. M. ([1999] 2012) *The Network Society*. 3rd edn, Thousand Oaks, CA: Sage.

van Dijk, J. A. G. M. (2013) Inequalities in the network society, in K. Orton-Johnson and N. Prior (eds), *Digital Sociology: Critical Perspectives*. Basingstoke: Palgrave Macmillan, pp. 105–24.

van Dijk, J. A. G. M., and van Deursen, A. J. A. M. (2014) *Digital Skills: Unlocking the Information Society*. New York: Palgrave Macmillan.

van Dijk, J. A. G. M., Peters, O., and Ebbers, W. (2008) Explaining the acceptance and use of government internet services: a multivariate analysis of 2006 survey data in the Netherlands, *Government Information Quarterly*, 25(3): 379–99.

van Dijk, J. A. G. M., and Hacker, K. L. (2003) The digital divide as a complex and dynamic phenomenon, *Information Society*, 19(4): 315–26.

van Dijk, J. A. G. M., and Hacker, K. L. (2018) *Internet and Democracy in the Network Society*. New York: Routledge.

van Laar, E., van Deursen, A. J. A. M., van Dijk, J. A. G. M., and de Haan, J. (2017) The relation between 21st-century skills and digital skills: a systematic literature review, *Computers in Human Behavior*, 72: 577–88.

Vecchione, M., and Caprara, G. V. (2009) Personality determinants of political participation: the contribution of traits and self-efficacy beliefs, *Personality and Individual Differences*, 46(4): 487–92.

Velleman, E. (2018) *The Implementation of Web Accessibility Standards by Dutch Municipalities: Factors of Resistance and Support.* PhD thesis, University of Twente.

Venkatesh, V., Morris, M. G., Davis, G. B., and Davis, F. D. (2003) User acceptance of information technology: toward a unified view, *MIS Quarterly*, 27(3): 425–78.

Volker, B., Andriessen, I., and Posthumus, H. (2014) Gesloten werelden? Sociale contacten tussen lager- en hogeropgeleiden [Closed worlds? Social contacts between people with high and low education], in M. Bovens, P. Dekker and W. L. Tiemeijer, *Gescheiden werelden? Een verkenning van sociaal-culturele tegenstellingen in Nederland.* The Hague: SCC and WRR, pp. 217–34.

Vuyk, K. (2017) *Oude en nieuwe ongelijkheid* [Old and new inequality]. Utrecht: Klement.

Wang, C.-H., McLee, Y., and Kuo, J.-H. (2011) Mapping the intellectual structure of digital divide, *International Journal of Social Science and Humanity*, 1(1): 49–54.

Wang, H., and Wellman, B. (2010) Social connectivity in America: changes in adult friendship network size from 2002 to 2007, *American Behavioral Scientist*, 53(8): 1148–69.

Warde, A., Wright, D., and Gayo-Cal, M. (2007) Understanding cultural omnivorousness: or, the myth of the cultural omnivore, *Cultural Sociology*, 1(2): 143–64.

Warschauer, M. (2003) *Technology and Social Inclusion: Rethinking the Digital Divide.* Cambridge, MA: MIT Press.

Warschauer, M., and Ames, M. (2010) Can one laptop per child save the world's poor? *Journal of International Affairs*, 64(1): 33–51.

Weber, M. ([1922] 1978) *Economy and Society.* Berkeley: University of California Press.

WEF (World Economic Forum) (2004–2018) *Global Information Technology* reports. Geneva: WEF.

Wehmeyer, M. (2004) Self-determination and the empowerment of people with disabilities, *American Rehabilitation*, 28(1): 22–9.

Wei, K.-K., Teo, H.-H., Chan, H. C., and Tan, B. C. Y. (2011) Conceptualizing and testing a social cognitive model of the digital divide, *Information Systems Research*, 22(1): 170–87.

Wellman, B., and Berkowitz, S. D. (eds) (1988) *Social Structures: A Network Approach.* Cambridge: Cambridge University Press.

WHO (World Health Organization) (2011) *World Report on Disability.* Geneva: WHO.

Witte, J. C., and Mannon, S. E. (2010) *The Internet and Social Inequalities*. New York: Routledge.

Wong, P.-K. (2002) ICT production and diffusion in Asia: digital dividends or digital divide? *Information Economics and Policy*, 14(2): 167–87.

World Bank (2016) *World Development Report 2016: Digital Dividends*. Washington, DC: World Bank.

Wright, E. O. (ed.) (2005) *Approaches to Class Analysis*. Cambridge: Cambridge University Press.

Wrzus, C., Hänel, M., Wagner, J., and Neyer, F. J. (2013) Social network changes and life events across the life span: a meta-analysis, *Psychological Bulletin*, 139(1): 53–80.

Wyatt, S., Henwood, F., Hart, A., and Smith, J. (2005) The digital divide, health information and everyday life, *New Media & Society*, 7(2): 199–218.

Yates, S., and Lockley, E. (2018) Social media and social class, *American Behavioral Scientist*, 62(9): 1291–316.

Yates, S., Kirby, J., and Lockley, E. (2015) Digital media use: differences and inequalities in relation to class and age, *Sociological Research Online*, 20(4): 1–21.

Zhang, X. (2013) Income disparity and digital divide: the internet consumption model and cross-country empirical research, *Telecommunications Policy*, 37(6–7): 515–29.

Zickuhr, K. (2011) *Generations and their Gadgets*. Washington, DC: Pew Internet & American Life Project.

Zillien, N. (2006) Soziale Ungleichheit in der Informations- und Wissensgesellschaft, in Zillien, *Digitale Ungleichheit: Neue Technologien und alte Ungleichheiten in der Informations- und Wissensgesellschaft*. Wiesbaden: Verlag für Sozialwissenschaften, pp. 29–69.

Zillien, N., and Hargittai, E. (2009) Digital distinction: status-specific types of internet usage, *Social Science Quarterly*, 90(2): 274–91.

Index

acceptance of technology theory 24–6, 30
access (physical)
  conditional 49, 50, 57, 60
  material 48–9, 60, 90–1,113, 121
access phases 2, 113, 134
  motivation/attitude 39–44
  physical 47–60
  skills 61–75, 135
  usage 80–92, 154–5
accessibility 43, 74–5, 112–13, 137, 153
adult education 54, 64, 69, 70, 71, 104,
  124, 126, 134, 138, 152, 153
Africa 54, 85, 87, 147
Americans 8, 42, 55, 89, 92, 104, 107, 124
age 42, 53–4, 72, 77, 86–7, 103, 106–8
artificial intelligence 114, 128–9, 130
attitudes to digital media 34–9, 113,
  149–50
augmented reality 49, 78, 114, 128–9, 130,
  157
automation 74, 75–6, 128–9, 130, 156
awareness programmes 140–1, 145, 150,
  152

Bonfadelli, Heinz 94,
Bourdieu, Pierre 27, 28, 118, 123
Brazil 55
broadband 48–9, 50, 53, 55–6, 75, 92,
  135, 142–3, 146–8, 151–2
Broadband Technology Opportunities
  Program 142
Bush administration 8–9, 142

Canada 142, 145
capacity of digital media 49, 55
China 11, 143–4
Clinton administration 9, 141
combined and uneven development 135,
  137, 146
community access centre (CAT) 135
community technology centre (CTC) 135,
  142

competency of digital media use 62–4
competition (market) 136–7, 149, 151,
  154, 156
computer anxiety 35, 38, 40, 43
computer driving licence 64, 153
costs of digital media 15, 27, 111, 113, 156
cultural capital 27–8, 40, 118–19, 120,
  123
cultural differentiation 28, 94–5, 123
cultural inequality 6, 16, 28, 123
cultural opportunities 100, 103
curriculum change 153
cyberabuse/cybercrime 105, 107–8

design of technology 55, 133, 152–3
developed countries 3, 6, 9–10, 29, 52–3,
  59–60, 85, 119, 135, 138, 141
developing countries 6, 9–10, 29, 52–3,
  59–60, 85, 135, 141, 145–8
developing strategy 146–7
diffusion of innovation theory 7–8, 15, 18,
  25–6, 58
digital divide
  critics 8–9
  definition 1–2, 7
  evolution 16, 46, 58–60, 62, 94–5,
    127–9, 130, 157
  history 2, 7–14
  level of research (first, second, third)
    7–14, 18, 47, 98
  metaphor 2–3
  perspectives 4–5, 134–41
  research 11, 17–23
  research disciplines 20–1
  research publications 22–3
  research questions 17–19
  research strategies 21–2
  research themes 19–21
  theory 23–33
digital literacy 5, 11, 62–5, 69, 93, 137–8
  see also digital skills; literacy
Digital New Zealanders 155